# learn to knit

## IN 50 SQUARES

A 2-in-1 knitting course and blanket pattern

ANNA PANTELOUS

DAVID & CHARLES
— PUBLISHING —

www.davidandcharles.com

# Contents

# Introduction

In recent years, many of my friends have asked me to teach them how to knit. Being an expat, I now live far away from most of them, so I decided to make a knitting course they could use.

My mother taught me to knit at a very early age. For the first few years, I would knit small squares to be used as doll blankets. My mother would oversee my work and I could run to her with every dropped stitch for immediate repair.

Adults, however, rarely have that luxury, and knitting miniature doll blankets is unlikely to interest them. Many people choose a garter stitch scarf for their very first project, which is not ideal either: the first half is often full of mistakes, and has a different tension to the second.

So, I needed to find an answer to a series of questions:

- How to teach an adult to knit, without having them knit endless useless samples before starting on a "real" project?
- What kind of project will look good while a beginner finds their bearings?
- How do you cover all the basic techniques in one project?

The modular structure of a patchwork blanket was the answer to these questions. Each square is just the right size for a beginner. It won't get boring, as a new technique is introduced with every square. The squares are also small enough to discard if first attempts are not good enough to include in the final project.

In this 2-in-1 knitting course and blanket pattern, I'll show you the techniques I use the most – but they are not the only way to do things. I encourage you to explore different techniques as you progress: observe other knitters, and use the internet and social media to find methods that suit you.

I hope you have as much fun knitting your blanket as I had designing it!

*Happy knitting!*

# HOW TO USE THIS BOOK

This book contains patterns for 50 knitted squares, each of which introduces you to a new technique. You can choose to knit them all in the order given, or you can pick and choose which ones to make. Under each square you will find some or all of the following headings:

### *YOU ALREADY KNOW HOW TO*

These are the skills required to knit each specific square. You may want to skip a square or two, or knit them in a different order. This section tells you if you have all the essential skills required for each square.

### EXTRA MATERIALS

For most of the squares you will need: a pair of knitting needles, DK or aran knitting yarn, a tapestry needle and a pair of scissors. If you need other materials, e.g., yarn in more than one colour, stitch markers, circular needles, double-pointed needles (DPNs) or a cable needle, you will find these listed in this section.

### NEW ABBREVIATIONS

Under this heading you will find any new abbreviations introduced for that square. The first abbreviations are introduced in square **04.** The Seedy One. For a complete list of the abbreviations used in this book, see Abbreviations.

## Instructions

In the instructions for each square you will find detailed explanations for the new technique**(s)**.

You can find supporting videos for a range of techniques at **www.bookmarkedhub.com**. Look out for the video symbol on some of the squares, at the top left or top right of the page. You can also go to the playlist by scanning the QR code on this page.

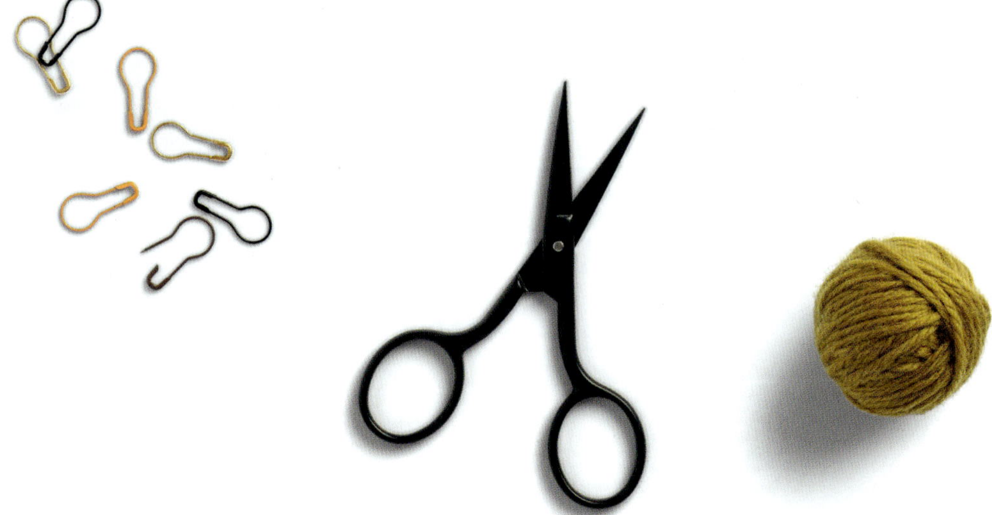

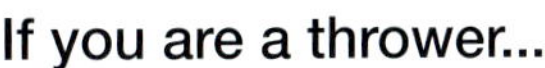

## Anna's tips...

These are my little secret tips for techniques I have found useful through the years.

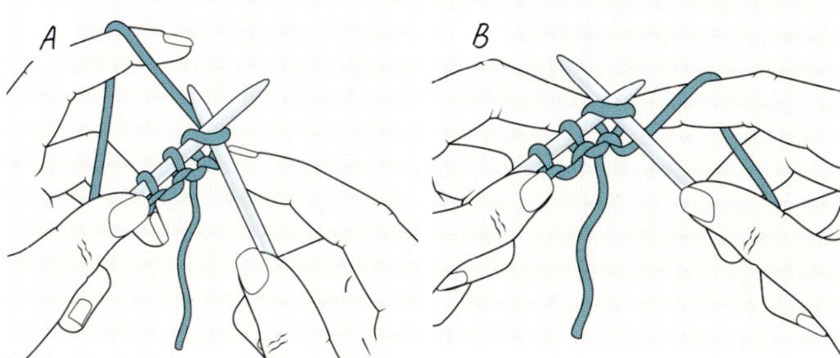


## GEEKY NOTES

This section contains extra information for those knitters who wish to know the hows and whys of a technique. You can skip this section if you wish.

## If you are a thrower...

There are two main schools of knitting, with some minor additional variations:

- holding the yarn in your left hand, known as "picking", or the Continental method **(A)**.
- holding the yarn in your right hand, known as "throwing", or English style **(B)**.

Both methods produce the same result, but use different movements to do so.

I am a picker myself, and believe this method has a couple of advantages over throwing. If you've never knitted before, I suggest you learn this method. However, if you have already learned to knit, even if it was a long time ago, you may choose to continue in the way you learned. You may think you've forgotten everything but, believe me, it's like riding a bike. Once you get started again, it will all come back to you.

Most of the techniques are similar for pickers and throwers. Where there are differences, this section will give details for throwers.

## A note on tension/gauge

Some knitters knit loosely, others tightly. Tension, or gauge, is a very personal thing.

This means that if you give two knitters the same yarn and needles, and ask them to knit a square using identical instructions, they may end up with squares of differing sizes.

When you read a pattern, you should not necessarily be looking at the specified needle sizes, but rather at the tension you need to achieve.

Tension shows you how dense your knitting is, i.e., how many stitches and rows you have in a square measuring 10 x 10cm/4 x 4in.

This number is of the utmost importance if you are knitting a garment, because a small difference in tension may translate into a much larger/smaller garment than intended.

In the case of an item like a scarf or a blanket, tension is not quite as important. However, you may want to experiment with different needle sizes until you get a fabric you are pleased with: neither too tight nor too loose, particularly the latter. A loose fabric does not work well with certain techniques, such as colourwork or entrelac.

## If you are left-handed

I've been asking left-handed knitters how they knit, and it turns out most of them knit the regular right-handed way.

I would recommend you do so too, if you are able, otherwise you will be knitting in the opposite direction to the majority, and you'll have to reverse all charts and instructions, which is not quite as obvious as it sounds.

I suggest you learn to pick, i.e. the Continental method, because the effort is more evenly distributed between the left and right hands.

I know a couple of people who have learned to knit the opposite way by mirroring the motions. If you wish to do so, you can watch tutorials through a mirror or you can make screen shots of photos and videos and use digital tools to flip the images horizontally.

## Blanket options

You can join the squares to make a full-size throw or baby blanket, depending on how many squares you make.

Each square measures approx. 15 x 15cm (6 x 6in).

For a full-size throw, I suggest you make 63 squares (7 x 9). For a baby blanket, I suggest 30 squares (5 x 6).

## Abbreviations

brk: brioche knit

brLsl dec: brioche left-leaning decrease

brRsl dec: brioche right-leaning decrease

brp: brioche purl

cn: cable needle

C6B: cable 6 back

C6F: cable 6 front

CDD: centred double decrease

CC: contrast colour

DC: dark colour

DPN(s): double-pointed needle(s)

DS: double stitch

k: knit

k2tog: knit 2 stitches together

kfb: knit front and back

kyok: knit, yarn over, knit into the same st

LC: light colour

LH: left hand

LI: left-leaning increase

LLI: left lifted increase

M1: make one increase

M1L: make one left

M1R: make one right

M1pL: make one purl left

M1pR: make one purl right

MC: main colour

p: purl

p2tog: purl two sts together

PM/SM/RM: place marker, slip marker from LH to RH needle/remove marker

RH: right hand

RI: right-leaning increase

RLI: right lifted increase

rnd(s): round(s)

RS: right side

SSK: slip, slip, knit (left-leaning decrease)

SSP: slip, slip, purl (left-leaning purl decrease)

sl: slip/slipped

sl1p: slip 1 stitch purlwise

sl1yo: slip one stitch purlwise + yarn over

st(s): stitch(es)

tbl: through the back loop

WS: wrong side

YO: yarn over

# TOOLS & MATERIALS

### TO START YOU WILL NEED:

- A pair of 4mm knitting needles (US size 6 or UK size 8)
- DK or aran (light or medium) knitting yarn
- A tapestry needle
- A pair of scissors

### LATER ON, YOU WILL NEED:

- DK or aran (light or medium) knitting yarn in more than one colour
- Stitch markers or scrap yarn tied in a loop. You will need a combination of removable and closed stitch markers (see **06.** The Mitred One).
- Size 4mm (US size 6 or UK size 8) circular needles, 40cm/16in long
- A set of 5 double pointed needles (DPNs), 4mm (US size 6 or UK size 8)
- A cable needle
- A 5mm (US size 6 or UK size H-8) crochet hook

### I'D ALSO RECOMMEND:

- A cup of tea or other drink (stay hydrated!)
- Good lighting
- Good music

### NICE-TO-HAVES:

- Kitchen scales (to weigh the yarn)
- A tape measure

## More specifically

### NEEDLES

I suggest you start with 4mm (US size 6 or UK size 8) needles. They are neither too thin nor too heavy. If you do choose another size, you will also need to choose your yarn accordingly (see Yarn).

Needles are made of a variety of materials: wood, plastic, bamboo or metal.

I am not particularly choosy – I will knit with almost any kind of needle. However, here are some things to look out for:

- Wooden or bamboo needles are pleasant to the touch and lighter than metal. If they are too thin (smaller than 3mm – US size 3 or UK size 10), I tend to break them.
- Some plastic needles are flexible, which I find terribly annoying.
- Some metal DPNs can be quite heavy and tend to fall out of the stitches. If you choose metal needles, go for the pale grey ones, which are made of light aluminium.
- Circular needles should have a smooth join between the needle and the cable, otherwise your stitches will keep catching at that point.
- If you are an absolute beginner, I would advise choosing short, straight needles (25.5cm/10in long) and learning the picking method. If, however, you are a thrower and you are used to supporting one needle under your arm, you should go for longer needles (up to 50cm/19in).

## YARN

Your choice of yarn depends on your choice of needles and vice versa. If you choose to knit the throw with 4mm (US size 6 or UK size 8) needles, you should be looking for DK or aran yarn, also called Yarn Group B or number 3. It should produce 18–21 stitches per 10cm/4in. For wool or cotton this usually means 100–140m (110–150yds) per 50g skein. Acrylic yarn is usually a bit lighter than that, so you get more length per skein.

My squares weigh between 14g and 18g each, depending on the pattern. This means I get approximately three squares per 50g skein of yarn. If you choose needles of a different size and yarn of a different weight to those I suggest, these numbers will be different.

There are many different kinds of yarn out there: some contain natural fibres (wool, cotton, linen, silk), others synthetic (acrylic, polyamide) and half-synthetic fibres (viscose, rayon, bamboo). For most purposes, and as a matter of principle, I prefer natural fibres.

Cotton or wool are wonderful fibres for a throw. Choose plain yarn if you are a beginner. Don't go for mohair or other very fluffy or fancy yarn – they may look great and feel nice, but they are not the best choices for a beginner who needs to be able to see what they are doing. I also advise keeping to one type of yarn if this is your first project.

If you are in a hot climate, cotton is a very good choice. Knitting with wool – or worse, acrylic – when you have sweaty hands is not much fun.

Given that you will need quite a few skeins to make all the squares, price might be a consideration. Acrylic yarn is usually less expensive than wool and is also moth-resistant.

You may also want to think about where the yarn is sourced: recycled yarns are widely available, as are cruelty-free and vegan alternatives.

Avoid black or very dark yarn in the beginning, as they make stitch details difficult to see.

This blanket is also a very good project for leftover yarn, if you have lots of small quantities of yarn. Just make sure they are of the same thickness, otherwise the result will be uneven and bumpy.

For my own throw, I used Soft Merino Aran from Rico Essentials, a lovely soft and squishy yarn with a good structure. I have used one main colour and one contrast colour, but you can go all out and combine any number of colours.

Do make sure to buy a yarn you like. You will (hopefully) be spending a lot of time with it in your hands!

*So, if you are ready to dive in, let's get started!* ☞

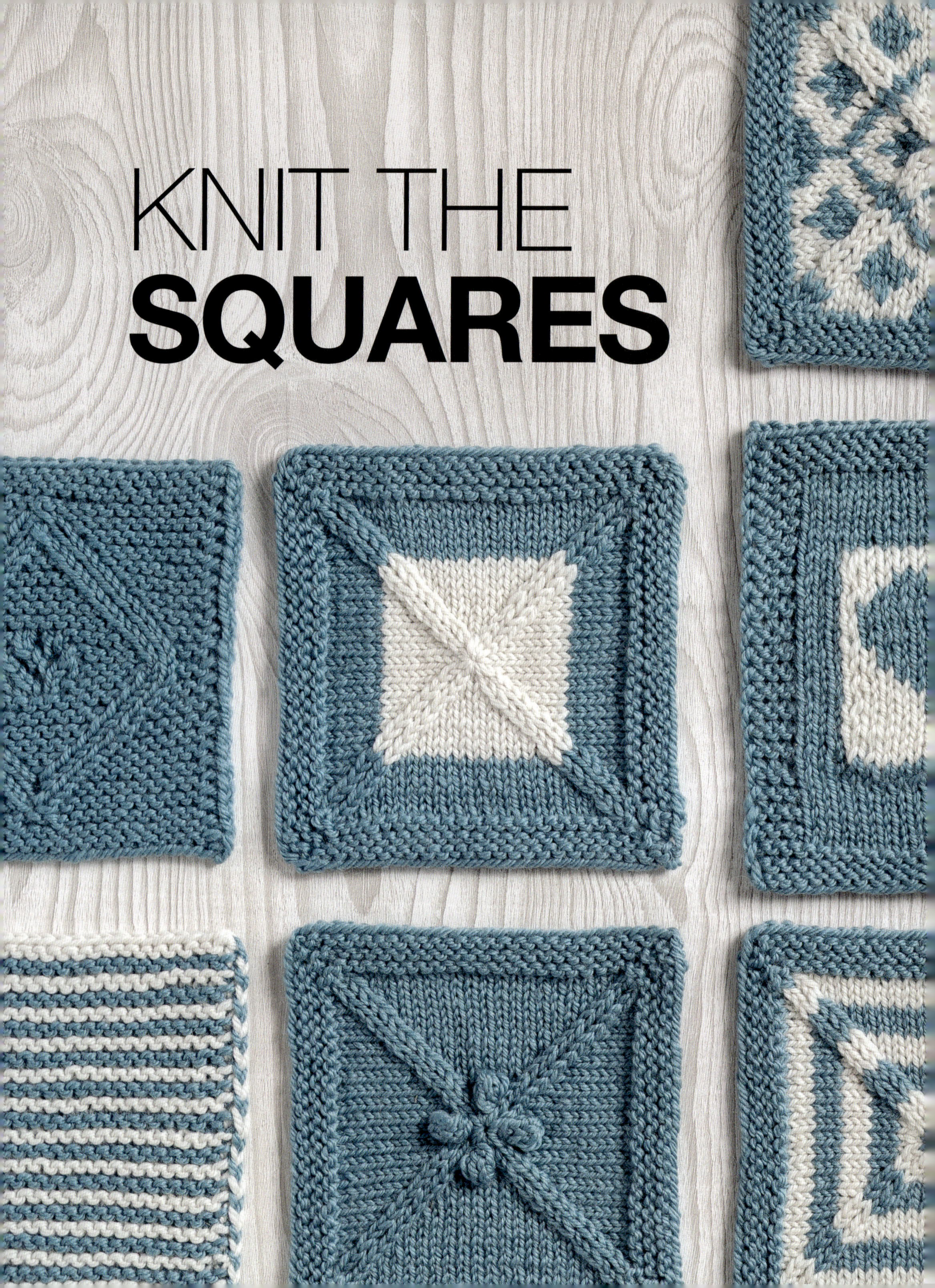
KNIT THE
SQUARES

See clips 00.1, 00.2, 00.3, 00.4.

# **00.** The Basic One

***How to work the long-tail cast on, make a knit stitch, and cast off***

If you already know how to cast on, cast (bind) off and work the knit stitch, I suggest you go directly to **01.** The Slippy One. If you have never knitted before, I suggest you start by knitting this square, which is not included in the blanket.

## Instructions

Leaving a yarn tail of approx 60cm (24in), make a slip knot and place it on a 4mm (US size 6 or UK size 8) knitting needle **(A, B, C)** with the yarn end in front and the working yarn (the yarn leading to the ball) to the back.

Hold the needle in your right hand. Place your left thumb and index finger between the two yarns and close your remaining fingers around the them. Open your thumb and index finger to form the so-called "slingshot" hold **(D)**.

Cast on another 26 stitches (27 stitches in total).

**To cast on a stitch:** insert the needle under the yarn on your thumb **(E)**, fetch the yarn on your index finger and pull it through the loop on your thumb **(F)**. Let go of the yarn on your thumb. Pull each stitch snug, but not tight, with your thumb **(G)** before casting on the next stitch.

After casting on the stitches, you should have a tail of minimum 10cm/4in left. Hold it together with the knitting needle in your left hand and just forget all about it for the time being. Make sure you don't start knitting with it!

Hold the yarn as shown in H, using your little finger to control the tension. Some people wrap the working yarn once or twice around their little finger. You will probably need to experiment a bit to find the way that works best for you.

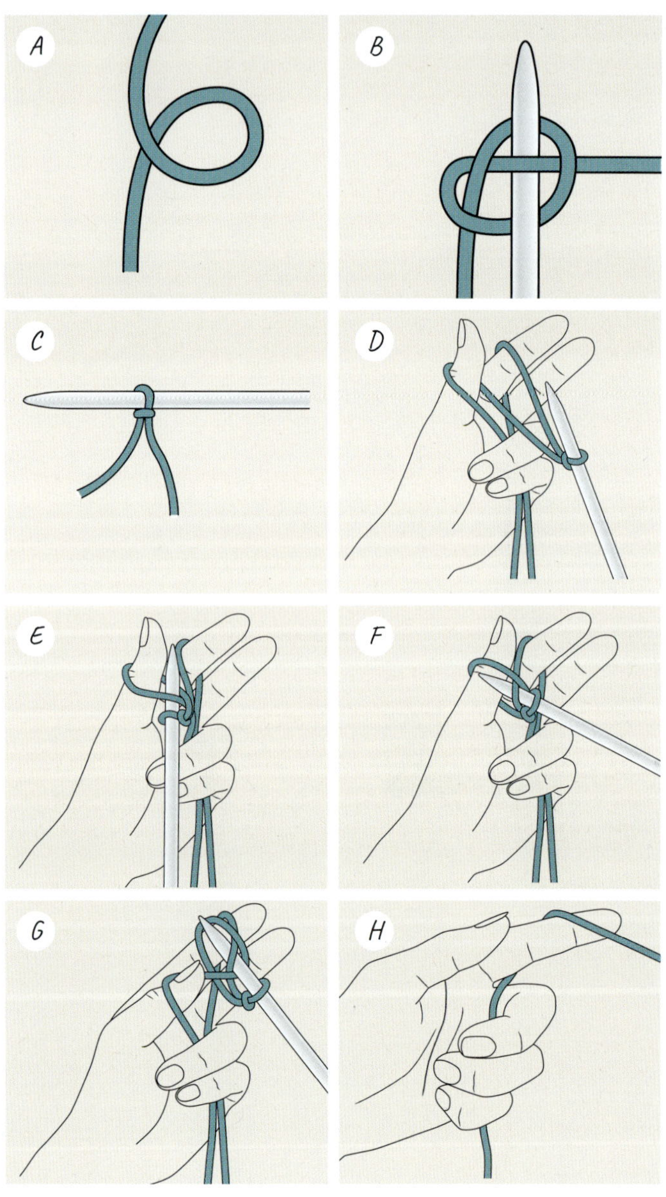

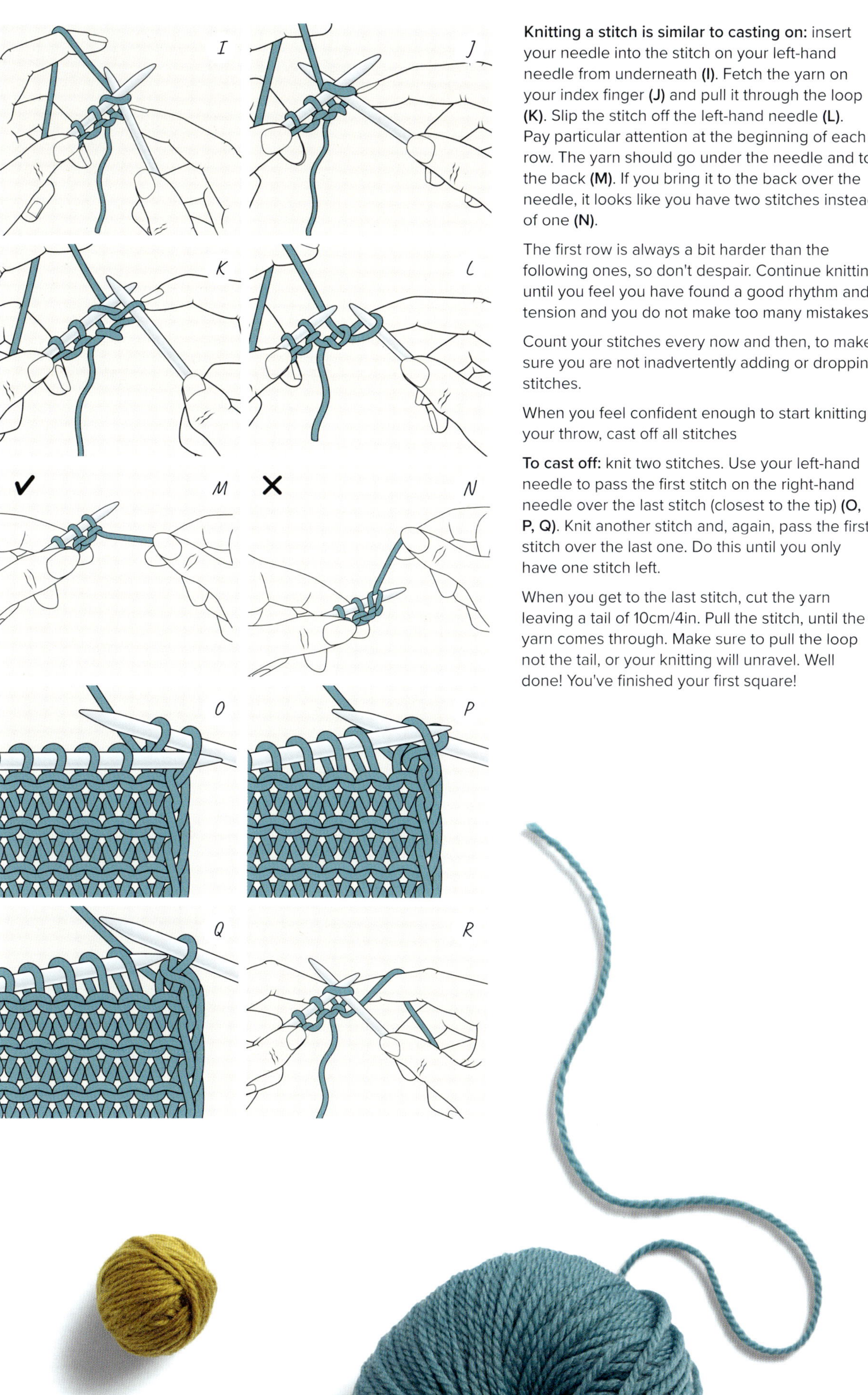


**Knitting a stitch is similar to casting on:** insert your needle into the stitch on your left-hand needle from underneath **(I)**. Fetch the yarn on your index finger **(J)** and pull it through the loop **(K)**. Slip the stitch off the left-hand needle **(L)**. Pay particular attention at the beginning of each row. The yarn should go under the needle and to the back **(M)**. If you bring it to the back over the needle, it looks like you have two stitches instead of one **(N)**.

The first row is always a bit harder than the following ones, so don't despair. Continue knitting until you feel you have found a good rhythm and tension and you do not make too many mistakes.

Count your stitches every now and then, to make sure you are not inadvertently adding or dropping stitches.

When you feel confident enough to start knitting your throw, cast off all stitches

**To cast off:** knit two stitches. Use your left-hand needle to pass the first stitch on the right-hand needle over the last stitch (closest to the tip) **(O, P, Q)**. Knit another stitch and, again, pass the first stitch over the last one. Do this until you only have one stitch left.

When you get to the last stitch, cut the yarn leaving a tail of 10cm/4in. Pull the stitch, until the yarn comes through. Make sure to pull the loop not the tail, or your knitting will unravel. Well done! You've finished your first square!

### If you are a thrower...

**To knit a stitch:** Insert your needle into the stitch on your left-hand needle from underneath **(R)**. Wrap the working yarn around the right-hand needle **(S)** and pull it through the loop **(T)**. Slip the stitch off the left-hand needle **(U)**.

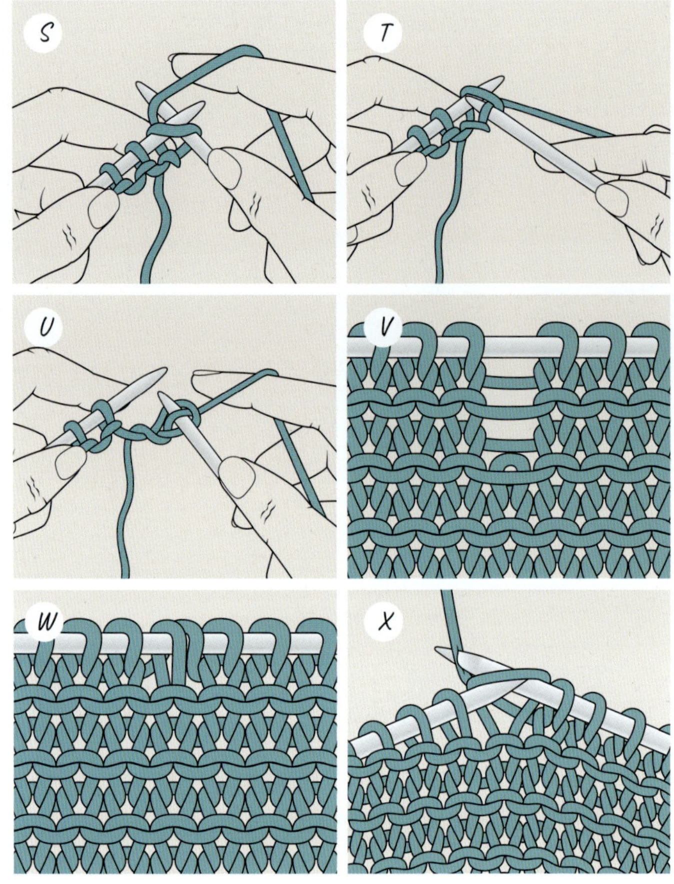


## GEEKY NOTES 

The pattern formed when you knit all the stitches in every row is called garter stitch.

It is also possible to start without a slip knot, but for the purposes of this blanket, all cast ons begin with one.

If you managed to complete this square, I suggest you move directly to the next one. You will have the opportunity to practise the techniques you have learned, and you will also learn how to slip the first stitch. Slipping the first stitch results in a smoother selvedge, which will make life easier for you when you come to assemble the squares.

*Anna's tips...* 

- Beginners tend to knit very tightly, which only makes it even more difficult. If you feel like a knight in a joust, you are probably too tense. Find a good posture and relax. The stitch you are knitting should be about 2cm/¾in from the tip of the needle. In time and with practise you will find the right tension.
- Do not put down your knitting while you are still in the middle of a row. Many mistakes happen because people stop in the middle of a row and pick up the needles the wrong way round when they resume.
- Count your stitches every few rows, to make sure you have the right number. Beginners often inadvertently add or drop stitches.
- Pay particular attention when starting a new row. I have seen many beginners turn the yarn the wrong way, thus adding an extra stitch at the beginning of each row. With practise, some movements will become automatic, so it is worth the effort to form good habits from the very beginning.
- Also look out for other common beginners' mistakes, including dropping stitches **(V)**, not pulling the yarn through the new stitch properly **(W)**, and splitting the yarn **(X)**.

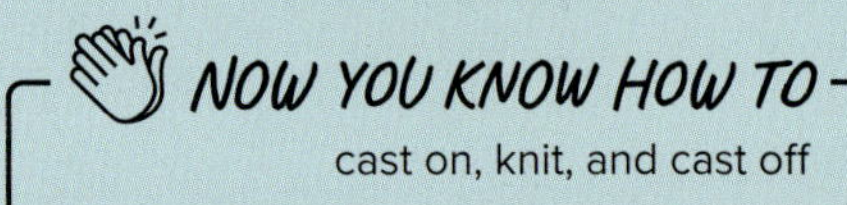

# **01.** The Slippy One

## *Slipped stitch*

With this square, you'll be learning how to slip the first stitch of every row purlwise. This will create a smooth selvedge, which will make life easier for you when you come to assemble the squares. It will also prepare you for the purl stitch.

See clips 01.1, 01.2.

### YOU ALREADY KNOW HOW TO

- cast on, knit, and cast/bind off (**00.** The Basic One)

## Instructions

Cast on 27 stitches.

Notice that when you cast on **(A)**, a ridge or wave is formed on the side of the work facing away from you **(B)**. This ridge should be on the wrong side of the work. This means that the first row you knit will be a wrong-side row.

**Row 1:** Slip the first stitch purlwise and knit the remaining 26 stitches.

**To slip the stitch:** go behind the working yarn with your needle and insert it into the first stitch from right to left **(C)**. Pull it off the needle **(D)**. Bring the right-hand needle behind the working yarn and to the right, to bring the working yarn into the correct position to knit your next stitch **(E)**.

The first time you slip the first stitch, hold your yarn firmly so that the stitch doesn't fall apart (and if it does, just cast it on again).

Notice that whenever you knit a row, a series of Vs is formed on the side facing you, and a ridge is formed on the side facing away from you.

**Row 2:** Slip the first stitch purlwise, knit the remaining 26 stitches.
**Rows 3–47:** As Row 2.

There should be 24 ridges on the right side of the square. This means you will have knitted 47 rows in total.

Cast off all stitches.

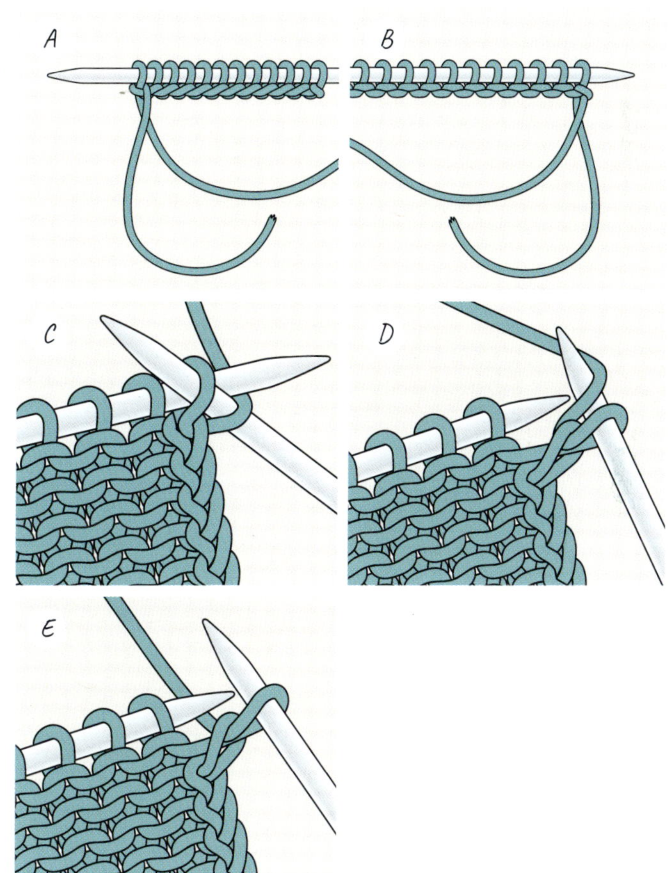

When you get to the last stitch, cut the yarn, leaving a tail of 10cm/4in. Pull this tail through the stitch.

Using a tapestry needle, weave in the ends diagonally on the wrong side. Follow the natural path of the stitches **(F)**.

You should weave in at least 5cm (2in) before cutting off the rest of the tail.

## If you are a thrower...

To slip the first stitch purlwise, the same principle applies: insert the needle behind your working yarn into the first stitch from right to left. Pull it off the left-hand needle. Turn the working yarn clockwise around your right-hand needle to bring it into position to knit the first stitch.

## GEEKY NOTES

### Why slip the first stitch?

When all stitches are knitted, the selvedge looks like a series of small knots **(G)**.

When slipping the first stitch, a chain is formed at the selvedge, making the pieces much easier to join **(H)**.

For pieces that do not need to be joined, it's a matter of personal preference: do you prefer the look of slipped or knitted stitches?

### What does purlwise mean?

When you knit a stitch, you insert the needle into the stitch from left to right. When you purl a stitch, you insert the needle from right to left, as you will see in **03**. The Purly One. So, if you slip a stitch by inserting the needle from right to left, this is called "slipping a stitch purlwise".

### Why the big maneouvre?

Slipping a stitch means transferring it from the left- to the right-hand needle without knitting it. That's simple enough. However, after slipping the first stitch purlwise, you have to bring the yarn into the correct position to knit the next stitch.

### *Anna's tips...*

- I like to cast on and cast off using a slightly larger needle than the ones I will be knitting with – in this case 4.5mm (US size and UK size 7) or 5mm (US size 8 and UK size 6).
- If you do not have a larger needle, another way to achieve the required slack is to leave 0.5cm/¼in between stitches.
- You may need to experiment until you find the perfect needle size and tension for your cast-on and cast-off edges.

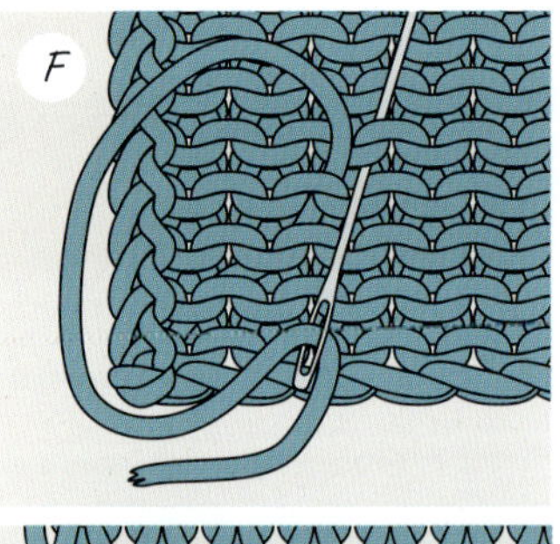

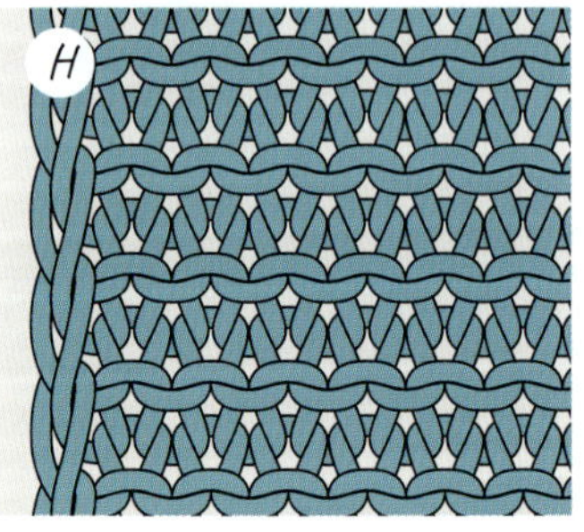

# **02.** The Striped One

## *How to knit horizontal stripes*

The first question I'm asked as soon as my students have learned to knit, is "How do I change colours?" Here's how to knit stripes.

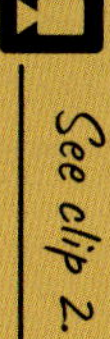

See clip 2.1.

- cast on, knit, and cast/bind off (**00.** The Basic One)
- slip the first stitch purlwise (**01.** The Slippy One)

### EXTRA MATERIALS

- yarn in 2 different colours

## Instructions

Cast on 27 stitches with the main colour.

**Row 1 (Wrong side):** Slip the first stitch purlwise, knit the remaining 26 stitches.
**Row 2 (Right side):** Slip the first stitch purlwise. Drop the main colour and pick up the contrast colour, knit the remaining 26 stitches with the contrast colour.
**Row 3:** Slip the first stitch purlwise, knit the remaining 26 stitches.
**Row 4:** Slip stitch purlwise. Drop the contrast colour and pick up the main colour without twisting the yarns **(A)**, knit the first stitch in the new colour loosely, otherwise the right side of the square will be too tight, knit the remaining 25 stitches.
**Row 5:** Slip stitch purlwise, knit the remaining 26 stitches.
**Rows 6–47:** Repeat Rows 4 and 5, alternating the colours on every other row.
You should have 24 ridges in total on the right side of your knitting.

Cast off and weave in ends.

In this square, you cannot weave the ends in diagonally as you normally would in garter stitch, because the yarn will be visible in the stripes of the contrasting colour. Weave in the ends into a single stripe **(B, C)** on the wrong side of the work.

Make extra squares with any combination of stripes you like!

## GEEKY NOTES

**Why change colour on the second stitch and not the first?**

Because the first stitch is slipped, not knitted. Were you to knit the first stitch, you would knit it in the new colour.

Notice that when changing colour, the ridges on the right side are single-coloured, while the ones on the wrong side are two-coloured.

Therefore, you should change colour when starting on a right-side row, unless you want precisely that effect, which I find particularly neat when changing between similar hues. This creates a smooth transition, like a continuous spectrum. In this case, you should change colour when starting a wrong-side row.

When changing colour every other row, as in this square, you do not need to break the yarn after every stripe. With wider stripes, however, you will have to break the yarn at every colour change, leaving a tail of approx 10cm/4in to weave in. This means you'll have a lot of loose ends to weave in!

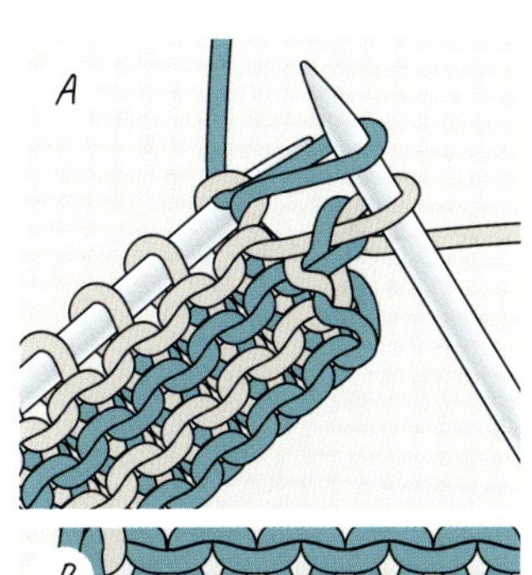


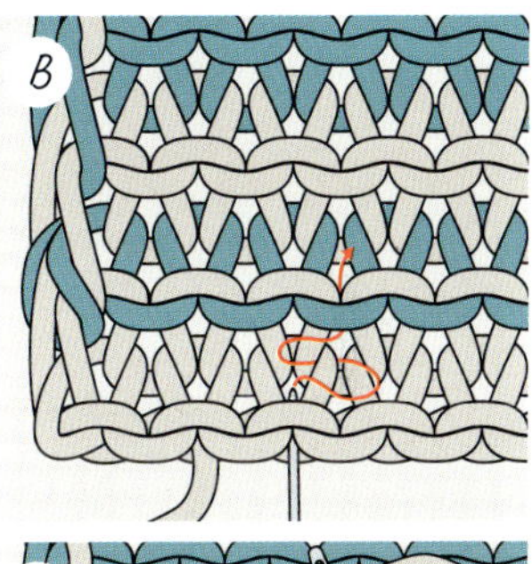


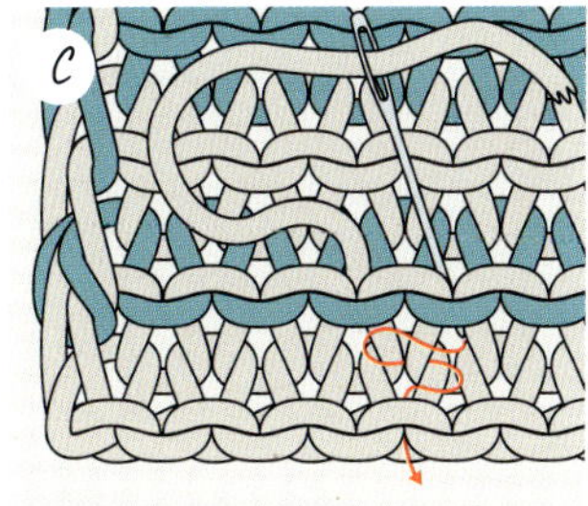

See clips 03.1, 03.2, 03.3.

# 03. The Purly One

## *How to purl*

There are two basic stitches in knitting: the knit stitch and the purl stitch. With this square, you will learn to purl. There are different ways of working the purl stitch. I use the Norwegian purl because you do not need to change the position of the working yarn between knit and purl stitches.

### YOU ALREADY KNOW HOW TO

- cast on, knit, and cast/bind off (**00.** The Basic One)
- slip the first stitch purlwise (**01.** The Slippy One)

## Instructions

Cast on 27 stitches.

**Rows 1–6:** Slip the first stitch purlwise, knit the remaining 26 stitches.

You have now 3 garter ridges on the right side of your knitting.

**Row 7 (Wrong side):** Slip the first stitch purlwise, knit 3 stitches, purl 19 stitches, knit 4 stitches.

**To purl a stitch:** go behind the working yarn and insert the right-hand needle into the stitch from right to left **(A)**. Move the needle upwards, towards the back and over the working yarn. Catch the working yarn **(B)** and bring it back through the stitch **(C)**. Slip the stitch off the left-hand needle **(D)**.

**Row 8:** Slip the first stitch purlwise, knit the remaining 26 stitches.
**Row 9:** Slip the first stitch purlwise, knit 3 stitches, purl 19 stitches, knit 4 stitches.

**Rows 10–41:** Repeat Rows 8 and 9 another 16 times.
At this point you should have 21 garter-stitch ridges in the garter-stitch border of the square.

**Rows 42–47:** Slip the first stitch purlwise, knit the remaining 26 stitches.

You now have 24 garter stitch ridges in the garter stitch border.

Cast off and weave in ends.

**To weave in the ends in stocking stitch:** work on the wrong side and follow the direction of the purl bumps. You do not need to move diagonally, just follow the direction of the yarn in a single row of knitting **(E, F)**.

### If you are a thrower...

To purl a stitch, you need to have the yarn in front of the work. This means you have to change the position of the yarn between knit and purl stitches.

With the yarn in front, insert the right-hand needle into the stitch from right to left **(G)**. Wrap the working yarn around the right-hand needle **(H)**, and pull it through the stitch **(I)**. Drop the stitch off the left-hand needle **(J)**.

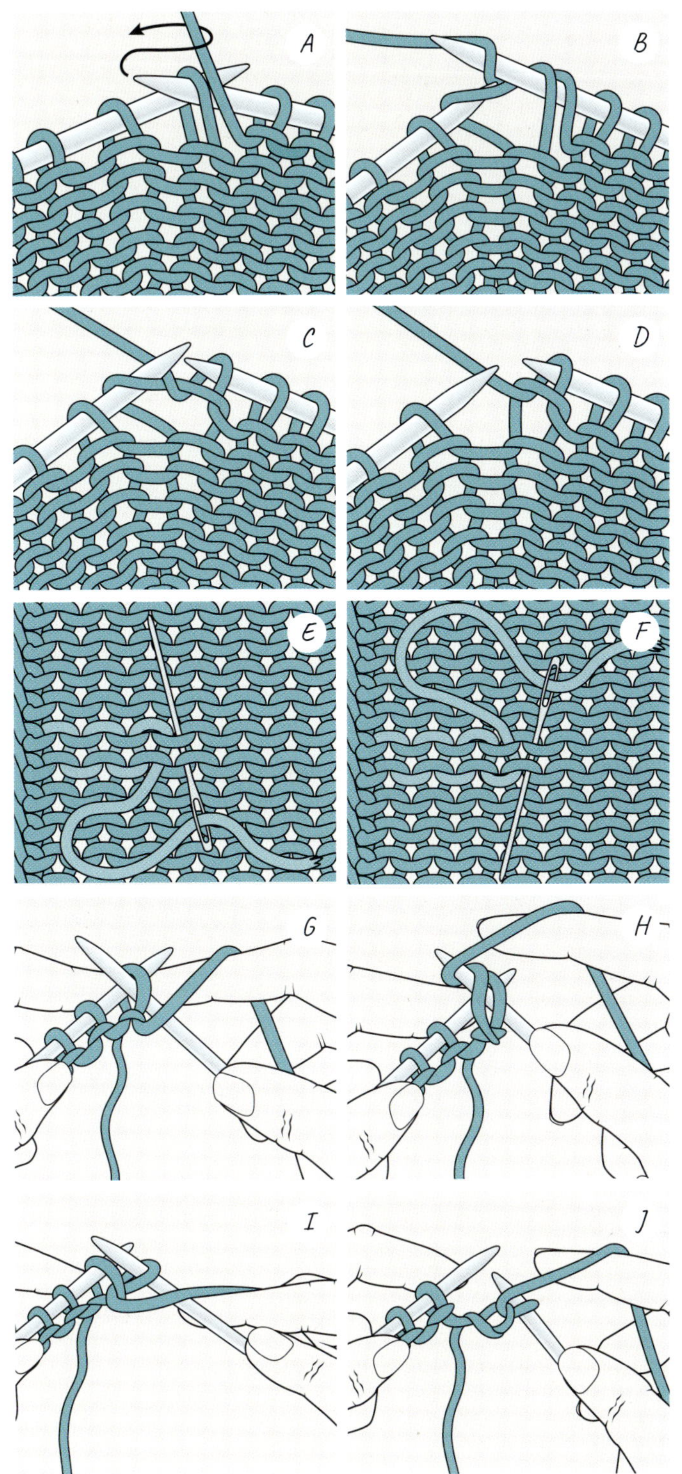


## GEEKY NOTES 

As mentioned already, whenever you knit a row, a series of Vs is formed on the side facing you, and a ridge is formed on the back. The opposite happens when you purl a row. By alternating knit and purl rows, you get all the Vs on one side and all the ridges on the other. This pattern is called "stocking" or "stockinette" stitch and is probably the most common knitting pattern.

If you knit a square entirely in stocking stitch, the top and bottom edges will roll inwards and the sides will roll outwards. This cannot be remedied, no matter how much you press it, so, in most cases, it is advisable to knit a border in another pattern such as garter, rib, or seed stitch (see **04.** The Seedy One).

Another way of purling is the Continental purl, where you bring the yarn to the front before purling a stitch. The purl movement is shorter, but you have to move the yarn back and forth between knit and purl stitches.

This square turns out a bit taller than the previous ones, but knitted fabrics are very forgiving. Each knitting pattern has its own texture and elasticity but, once joined, the squares will pull each other into shape. However, I do take the length of the squares into account when planning their placement. If you want to plan the placement in advance, see Placement.

This square can also be made with stripes. Change colours as in **02.** The Striped One.

Knitting and purling are the two main stitches in knitting. Congratulations on learning to purl!

*NOW YOU KNOW HOW TO*

purl

See clip 04.1, 04.2.

# **04.** The Seedy One

## *How to follow a knitting pattern containing abbreviations*

Most knitting patterns use abbreviations to save space and to make them easier to read, so it's a good idea to get acquainted with the most common abbreviations. This square features a common pattern called "moss" or "seed" stitch. It's worked by alternating knit and purl stitches.

### YOU ALREADY KNOW HOW TO

- cast on, knit, and cast/bind off (**00**. The Basic One)
- slip the first stitch purlwise (**01.** The Slippy One)
- purl (**03**. The Purly One)

### NEW ABBREVIATION

**k:** knit, e.g., k26 means "knit 26 stitches"
**p:** purl, e.g., p1 means "purl 1 stitch"
**sl:** slip/slipped
**sl1p:** slip 1 stitch purlwise
**st(s):** stitch(es)
**[ ]:** repeat instructions within square brackets a specified number of times, e.g., [k1, p1] 3 times, means "knit 1 stitch, purl 1 stitch, knit 1 stitch, purl 1 stitch, knit 1 stitch, purl 1 stitch"

## Instructions

Cast on 27 sts.

**Rows 1–6:** Sl1p, k26.

Remember that Row 1 is a wrong-side row.

**Rows 7–41:** Sl1p, k3, [p1, k1] 9 times, p1, k4.
**Rows 42–47:** Sl1p, k26.

Cast off and weave in ends.

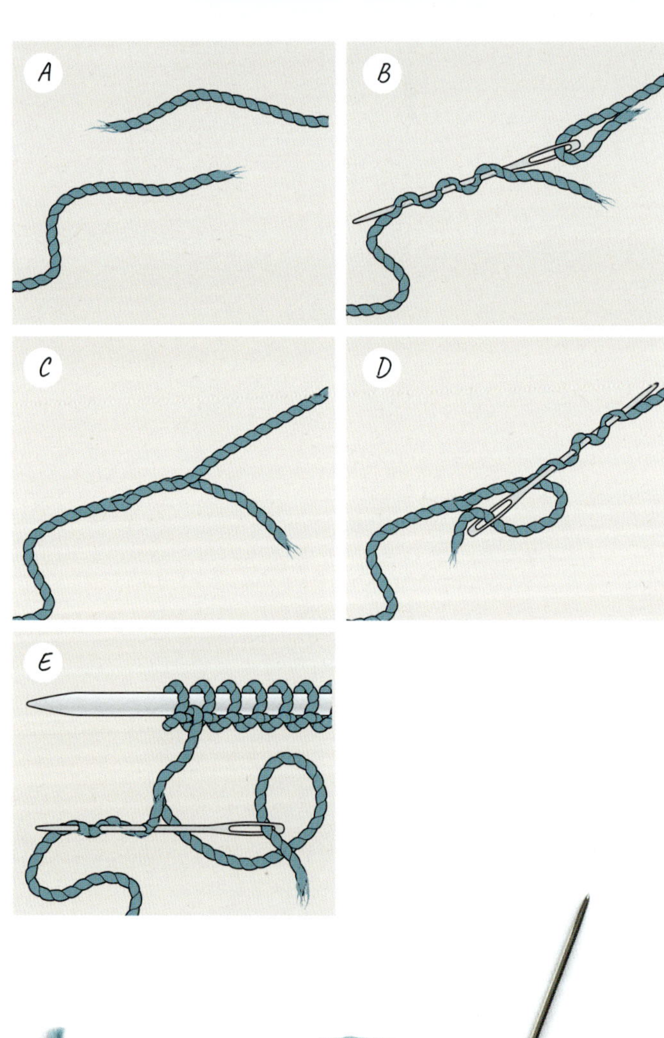

## Anna's tips...

### HOW TO JOIN SKEINS

At some point, you will come to the end of your skein. If you are in the middle of a square, you will need to join a new skein.

Some people tie knots, but I belong to the no-knots-allowed-in-knitting school.

My preferred way of joining skeins is by sewing one yarn end into the other. Taper the ends first, either by pulling and breaking the yarn or by fraying the ends with a scissor blade **(A)**. Thread one yarn end through a tapestry needle, and pull between the plied strands of the other end **(B)**. Pull both pieces of yarn lightly, so that the end settles snugly between the plies **(C)**. Repeat with the other end **(D)**.

- If you are knitting with wool or another natural fibre, you can make the join even smoother by rubbing it between your hands. The moisture will felt the yarn. This is known as "spit-splicing", but you don't have to take that literally – you can use a drop of tap water.
- I like to weave in the first end in advance, by sewing it into the working yarn **(E)**. This way I can reduce the number of ends I have to weave in at the end.
- When you use more than one skein of the same colour for a project, you should be aware of lot numbers. Each dye lot of yarn gets a number. The colour of the different lots may differ significantly, which means that if you combine different dye lots in a project, you may get visible lines at the places where you change skeins. For this project, I suggest you do not change lot numbers within a square. Using different lots in different squares should not be a problem, though.

**NOW YOU KNOW HOW TO**

follow a knitting pattern containing abbreviations

See clip 05.1, 05.2, 05.3.

# 05. The Charted One

## *How to read a knitting chart*

Some knitting patterns include charts, so reading a chart will be a useful skill to learn.

### YOU ALREADY KNOW HOW TO

- cast on, knit, and cast/bind off (**00**. The Basic One)
- slip the first stitch purlwise (**01**. The Slippy One)
- purl (**03**. The Purly One)
- follow a knitting pattern containing abbreviations (**04**. The Seedy One)

### NEW ABBREVIATIONS

**RS:** right side
**WS:** wrong side

## Instructions

The chart shows the RS of the knitting. Each square represents a stitch.

The chart is designed to represent how the knitting appears when looked at from the RS. This means that if an empty square means to knit on a RS row, it means to purl it on a WS row, and vice versa. As in the previous squares, always slip the first st purlwise.

Remember that the RS of your square (the one meant to be seen) is the one facing you when the cast-on tail is at the bottom left, and that Row 1 is a WS row. All odd-numbered rows (WS rows) are to be read from left to right and all even numbered rows (RS rows) are to be read from right to left. Start at the bottom left of the chart.

This square is perfectly symmetrical, so it won't make much of a difference, but for non-symmetrical charts, this is very important!

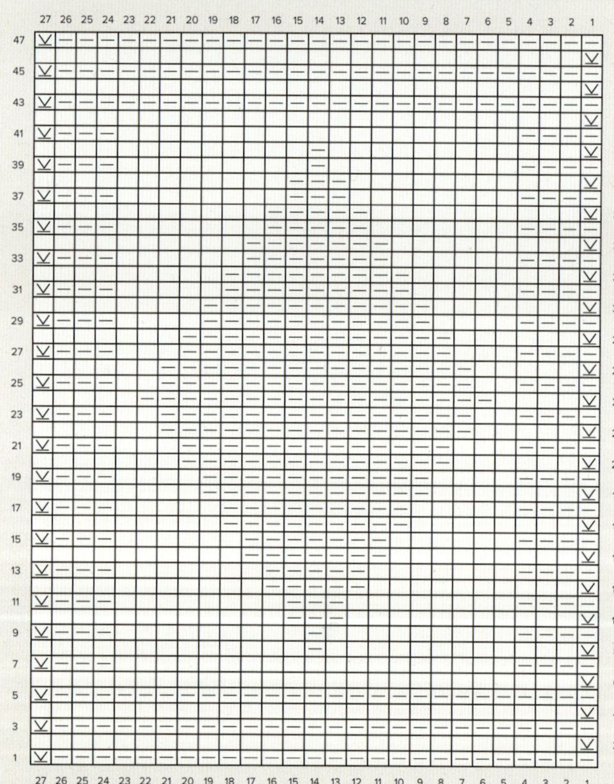


### CHART KEY

☐ RS: k / WS: p
⊟ RS: p / WS: k
☒ Sl1p

## *Anna's tips...*

- You can use a piece of cardboard to cover up part of the chart to keep track of the row you are knitting. Cover up the rows above – not below – the one you are knitting. That way, what you are seeing on your chart will correspond to what you can see on your knitting.
- Did you make a mistake a few stitches back and need to correct it? You can un-knit stitches. To do this: insert the left-hand needle into the stitch below the stitch on the right-hand needle **(A)**. Drop the stitch off the right-hand needle **(B)** and pull the yarn slightly to release the loop **(C)**. This is also known as tinking: T-I-N-K is K-N-I-T backwards – get it?
- Did you drop a stitch? Use a crochet hook to pick it up again. To pick up a knit stitch, insert the crochet hook into the stitch from front to back, catch the horizontal strand and pull it through the stitch **(D)**. To pick up a purl stitch, insert the crochet hook into the stitch from back to front, catch the horizontal strand and pull it through the stitch **(E)**. If you are picking up a stitch in garter stitch, you have to alternate between the two. When placing the stitch back on the left needle, make sure to have the right leg in front.

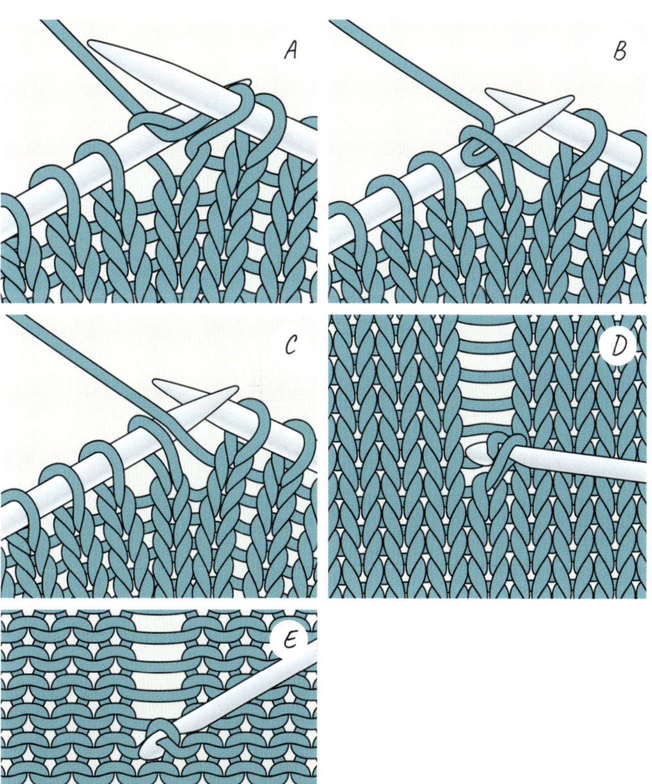


Cast on 27 sts.

Work according to chart as follows:

**Rows 1–6:** Sl1p, k26.
**Row 7 (WS):** Sl1p, k3, p19, k4.
**Row 8 (RS):** Sl1p, k12, p1, k13.
**Row 9 (WS):** Sl1p, k3, p9, k1, p9, k4.
**Row 10 (RS):** Sl1p, k11, p3, k12.
**Row 11 (WS):** Sl1p, k3, p8, k3, p8, k4.
**Rows 12–47:** Continue according to chart.

Cast off and weave in ends.

### GEEKY NOTES

There are several different knitting symbol systems. Furthermore, the same symbol may signify different stitches in different charts. Most charts therefore include a key to the symbols. Make sure to check it out!

# 06. The Mitred One

### *How to knit two stitches together and how to use stitch markers*

Up to now you have learned how to knit squares or rectangles, but of course there's much more to knitting than that. If you want to make strange shapes like sleeves or necklines, you need to add or eliminate stitches. With this square you will learn the most basic decrease.

## YOU ALREADY KNOW HOW TO

- cast on, knit, and cast/bind off (**00**. The Basic One)
- slip the first stitch purlwise (**01.** The Slippy One)
- follow a knitting pattern containing abbreviations (**04**. The Seedy One)

## EXTRA MATERIALS

- 1 stitch marker

## NEW ABBREVIATIONS

**k2tog:** knit 2 stitches together (i.e., decrease 1 stitch)
**LH:** left hand
**RH:** right hand
**PM/SM/RM:** place marker/slip marker from LH to RH needle/remove marker

## Instructions

Cast on 48 sts.
**Row 1 (WS):** Sl1p, k23, PM on RH needle **(A)**, k24.
**Row 2 (RS):** Sl1p, k to marker, SM, k2tog, k to end of row. (1 st decreased)

**To make a k2tog:** knit 2 sts together as if they were a single st **(B)**.

**Rows 3–45:** As Row 2. (4 sts)
**Row 46 (RS):** Sl1p, k1, RM, k2tog. (3 sts)
**Row 47 (WS):** Sl1p, k2tog. (2 sts)
**Row 48 (RS):** K2tog.

Break the yarn and pull it through the last st. Weave in the ends.

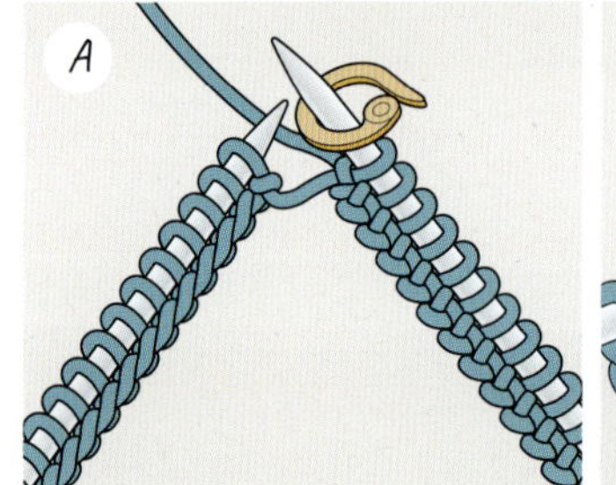


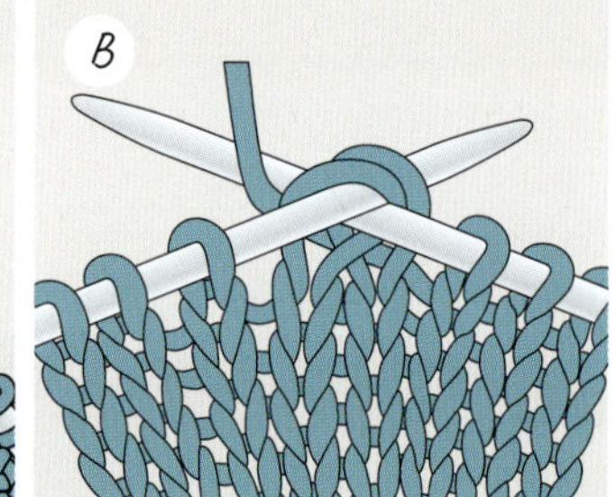


### Anna's tips...

I had been knitting happily for 40 years before I discovered you could buy stitch markers. I just used a length of scrap yarn. That said, they are quite convenient, but you don't have to rush out to buy them. You probably have lots of items around the house that can be used: rings, earrings (just make sure they have no snags!), small safety pins, paper clips, the small rings that come with electric toothbrushes or – my personal favourite – the small metal or plastic rings found on bras and swimwear.

There are two categories of stitch marker:

- removable stitch markers are like safety pins, so you can clip them onto your knitted fabric and remove them at any time
- closed stitch markers are small rings that you can slip onto your knitting needles. These need to be removed before you cast off, or you won't be able to get them out again...

## Variation

This square can also be made with stripes. The stripes accent the mitred structure. Change colours as in **02.** The Striped One. I like to use this square for the corners of my blanket.



NOW YOU KNOW HOW TO

decrease by knitting two stitches together

place and slip a marker

# 07. The Holey One

## *How to make a yarn over*

There are many different ways to increase your working stitches. The easiest is the yarn over, which creates a hole and is therefore often used in lacy patterns. By combining a yarn over with a decrease, you can make eyelets without increasing your stitches.

### YOU ALREADY KNOW HOW TO

- cast on, knit, and cast/bind off (**00**. The Basic One)
- slip the first stitch purlwise (**01.** The Slippy One)
- purl (**03**. The Purly One)
- follow a knitting pattern containing abbreviations (**04**. The Seedy One)
- read a knitting chart (**05**. The Charted One)
- decrease by knitting two stitches together (**06**. The Mitred One)

### NEW ABBREVIATIONS

**YO:** yarn over

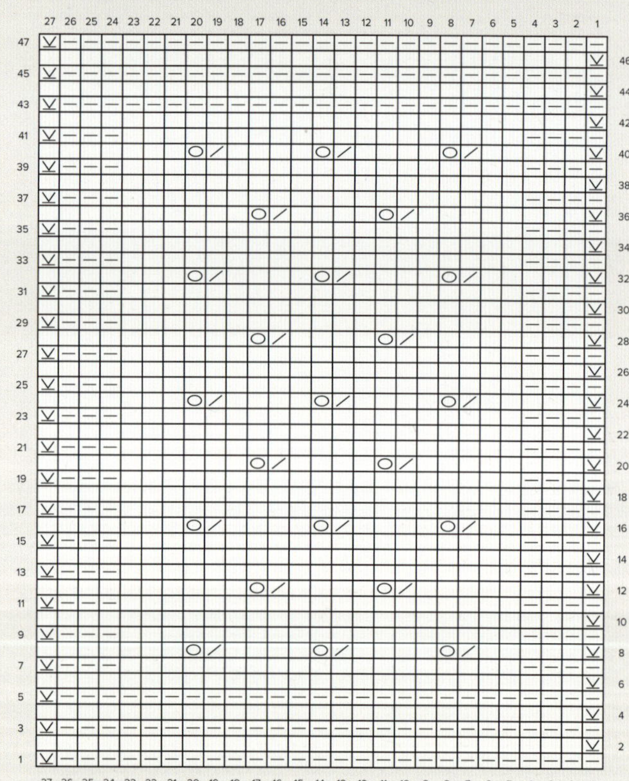

### CHART KEY

- ☐ RS: k / WS: p
- ⧄ k2tog
- ⊟ RS: p / WS: k
- ☑ Sl1p
- ◙ YO

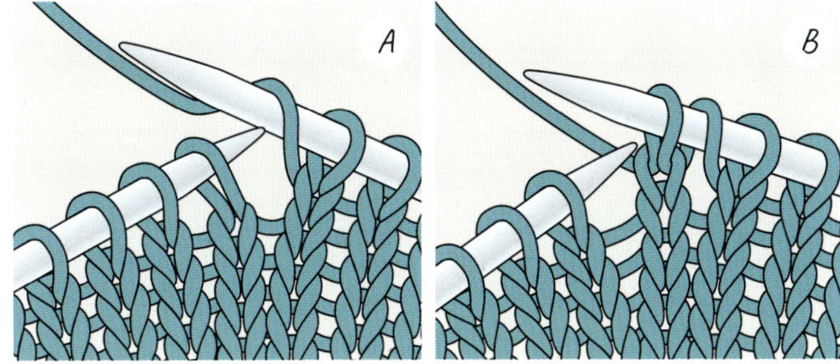


## Anna's tips...

To frog, or not to frog? That is the question.

You've just discovered a mistake you made a few rows back and you are really annoyed. You don't want to unravel (also known as frogging, because you "rip it, rip it").

If you are just learning to knit, I would advise you not to be too much of a perfectionist. In the very beginning, it's more important to find the right rhythm and tension. Be proud of your first project, even if it contains mistakes!

In certain cultures, flawless handicrafts are considered hubristic, or are believed to trap your soul. Deliberate mistakes are introduced to avoid such a great sin or calamity!

On the other hand, you might as well get used to the idea that discarding and undoing are an essential part of the creative process. Believe me, I hate having to undo several hours' or days' work, but these seemingly wasted hours are not really wasted: they are part of the process, and they will soon be forgotten, while you will hopefully cherish and enjoy your finished projects for many years to come.

Deciding if and when to correct mistakes is tricky!

# Instructions

Cast on 27 sts.

Work according to chart as follows:

**Rows 1–6:** Sl1p, k26.
**Row 7 (WS):** Sl1p, k3, p19, k4.
**Row 8 (RS):** Sl1p, k5, k2tog, YO, k4, k2tog, YO, k4, k2tog, YO, k7.

**To make a yarn over:** wrap the yarn around your LH needle **(A)**. Work the next st as you normally would **(B)**. The yarn over is worked as a regular st in the next row.

At this point it would be a good idea to check that you still have 27 sts on your needles.

**Row 9 (WS):** Sl1p, k3, p19, k4.
**Rows 10–47:** Continue according to chart.

Cast off and weave in ends.

## If you are a thrower...

The yarn needs to be in front of your work before you start the yarn over, so:

- if you have just knitted a st, bring the yarn to the front and then over the RH needle to the back.
- if you have just purled a st, the yarn is already in front, so you just need to bring it over the RH needle to the back.
- if your next st after the yarn over is a knit st, you are fine and good to go.
- if your next st is a purl st, you have to bring the yarn to the front again.

See clip 08.1

# **08.** The Left One

## *How to make a left-leaning decrease*

When you knit two stitches together you get a right-leaning decrease. If you want to have symmetrical decreases, you can make a right-leaning decrease on one side but will then need a left-leaning decrease for the opposite side.

### YOU ALREADY KNOW HOW TO

- cast on, knit, and cast/bind off (**00**. The Basic One)
- slip the first stitch purlwise (**01**. The Slippy One)
- purl (**03**. The Purly One)
- follow a knitting pattern containing abbreviations (**04**. The Seedy One)
- read a knitting chart (**05**. The Charted One)
- decrease by knitting two stitches together (**06**. The Mitred One)
- make a yarn over (**07**. The Holey One)

### NEW ABBREVIATIONS

**SSK:** slip, slip, knit (left-leaning decrease)

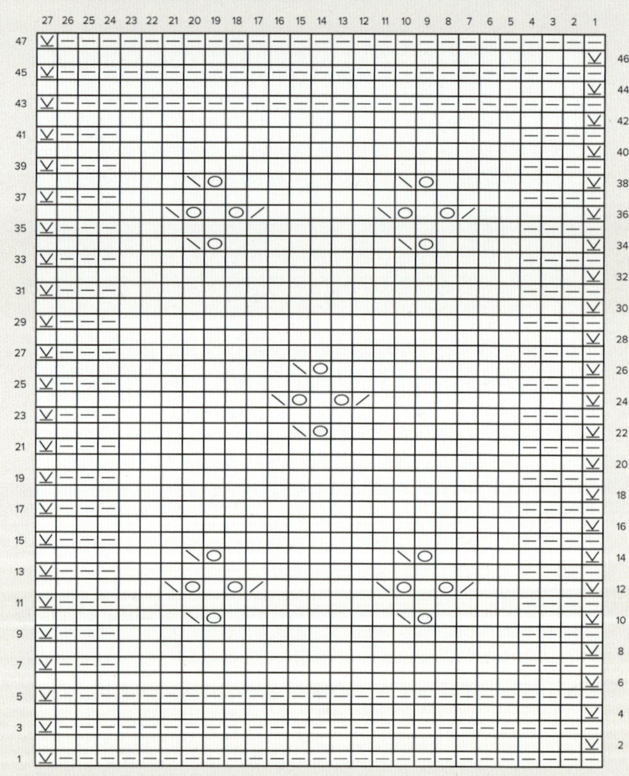


### CHART KEY

- RS: k / WS: p
- K2tog
- RS: p / WS: k
- Sl1p
- SSK
- YO

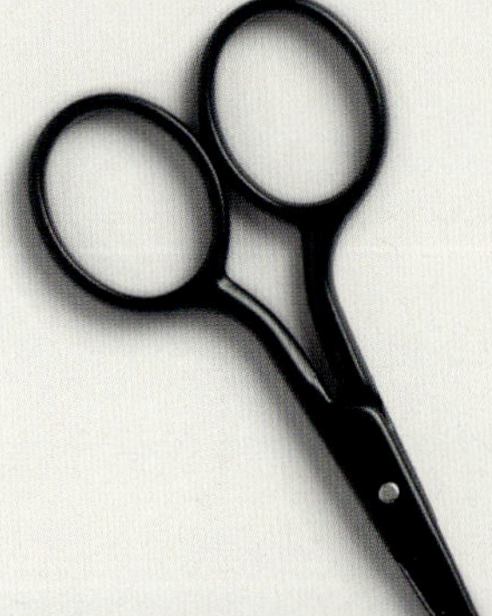

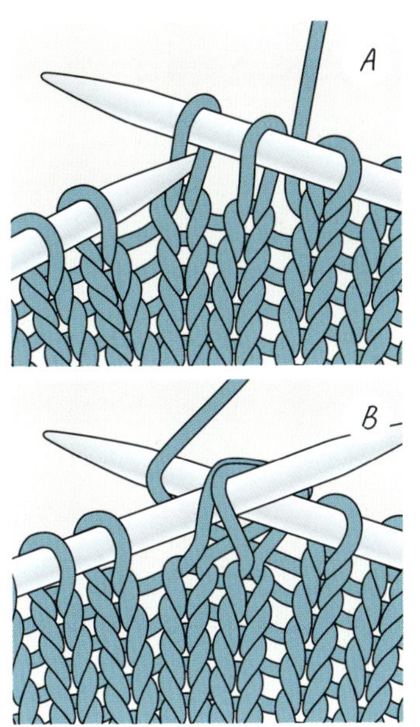


## Instructions

Cast on 27 sts.

Work according to chart as follows:

**Rows 1–6:** Sl1p, k26.
**Row 7 (WS):** Sl1p, k3, p19, k4.
**Row 8 (RS):** Sl1p, k26.
**Row 9 (WS):** As Row 7.
**Row 10 (RS):** Sl1p, k7, YO, SSK, k8, YO, SSK, k7.

**To make a SSK:** sl 1 st knitwise, sl the next st knitwise **(A)**, insert LH needle into 2 sl sts **(B)** and knit them together.

At this point it is a good idea to check that you still have 27 sts on your needle.

**Row 11 (WS):** Sl1p, k3, p19, k4.
**Rows 12–47:** Continue according to chart.

Cast off and weave in ends.

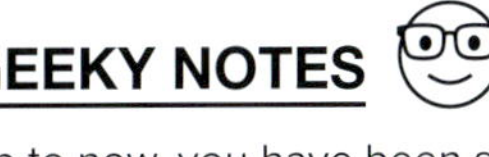


Up to now, you have been slipping stitches purlwise. In some cases, as in left-leaning decreases, stitches should be slipped knitwise, i.e., insert the RH needle into the stitch from left to right as if to knit the stitch, and slip it off the LH needle.

There are two basic ways of making a left-leaning decrease:

- **SSK (slip, slip, knit):** sl 1 st knitwise, sl the next st knitwise, insert LH needle into the front of the 2 sl sts and knit them together
- **Skpo/Skp (slip, knit, pass slipped st over):** sl 1 st, knit next st, pass the sl st over the knitted st (as you do when casting off)

Structurally, the result is the same. However, Skpo allegedly gives a more defined result, which is usually the desired effect in lacy patterns, while SSK gives a smoother result, which is ideal when decreasing for armholes or a neckline. I have to admit that I cannot tell the difference in my own knitting, but I suppose that it depends a lot on the yarn and the knitter.

Some people like to twist the stitch that lies below, because allegedly this produces a smoother result. This is known as the “improved SSK”, but this stitch does not accurately mirror the structure of the k2tog and I cannot bear the thought...

In short, I always do a SSK, but every knitter is different. I can only encourage you to try out different methods and choose what works best for you!

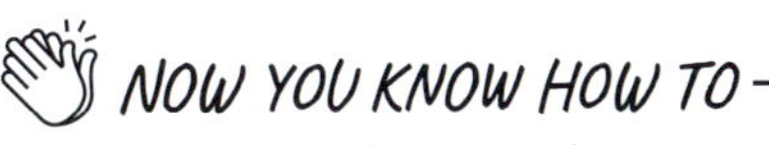


make a left-leaning decrease
slip a stitch knitwise

See clips 09.1, 09.2

# **09.** The Twisted One

## *How to knit or purl a stitch through the back loop*

Twisted stitches stand out against the background and have a more defined look. They are often used in intricate designs.

### YOU ALREADY KNOW HOW TO

- cast on, knit, and cast/bind off (**00**. The Basic One)
- slip the first stitch purlwise (**01**. The Slippy One)
- purl (**03**. The Purly One)
- follow a knitting pattern containing abbreviations (**04**. The Seedy One)
- read a knitting chart (**05**. The Charted One)

### NEW ABBREVIATIONS

**tbl:** through the back loop

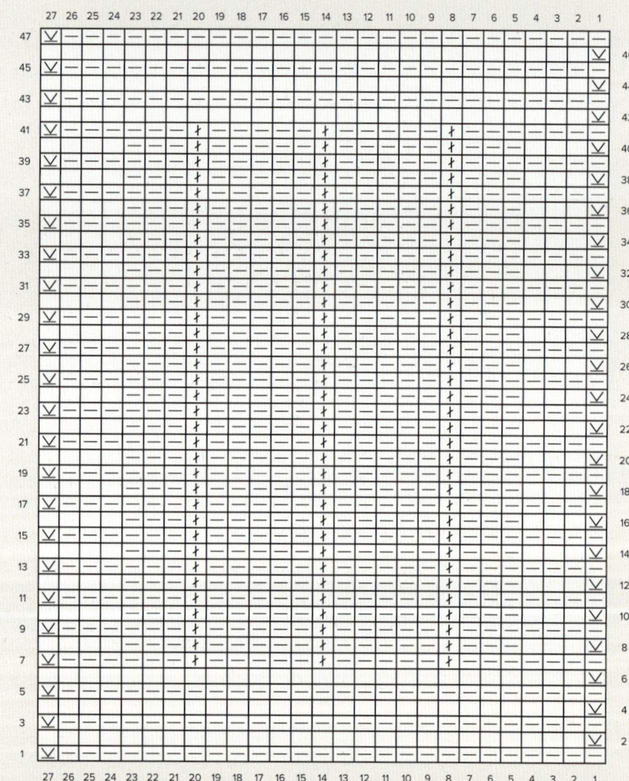

### CHART KEY

- RS: k / WS: p
- RS: k1 tbl / WS: p1 tbl
- RS: p / WS: k
- Sl1p

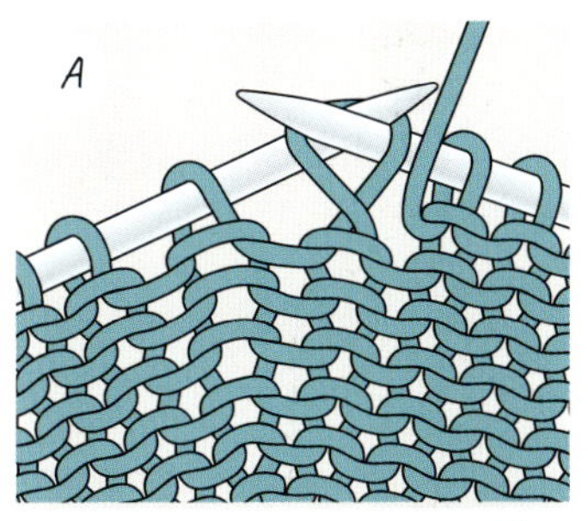


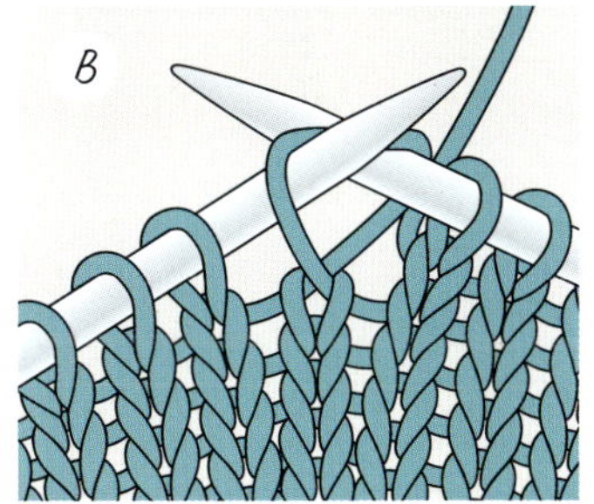


## Instructions

Cast on 27 sts.

**Rows 1–6:** Sl1p, k26.
**Row 7 (WS):** Sl1p, k6, [p1 tbl, k5] twice, p1 tbl, k7.

**To purl a st through the back loop:** insert your needle into the st from behind, i.e., pick up the back leg **(A)**. Complete the st as you would a normal purl st.

**Row 8 (RS):** Sl1p, k3, p3, [k1 tbl, p5] twice, k1 tbl, p3, k4.

**To knit a st through the back loop:** insert your needle into the st purlwise **(B)** and knit the back leg.

**Rows 9–40:** Repeat rows 7 and 8 another 16 times.
**Row 41 (WS):** As Row 7.
**Rows 42–47:** Sl1p, k26.

Cast off and weave in ends.

## GEEKY NOTES

When stitches are mounted correctly on the needle, the right leg of the stitch is positioned in front of the needle, and this is the leg you typically knit into. Knitting through the back loop crosses the legs of the stitch, which results in a tighter, more defined stitch that stands out more prominently on the fabric.

knit and purl a stitch through the back loop

See clip 10.1

# 10. The Diagonal One

## *How to make a kfb increase*

In square **07.** The Holey One you learned how to make a yarn-over increase. But, as already mentioned and as you probably saw yourself, that increase leaves a hole. One way of increasing without leaving a big hole is to knit the same stitch twice: first the normal way and then through the back loop.

### YOU ALREADY KNOW HOW TO

- cast on, knit, and cast/bind off (**00**. The Basic One)
- slip the first stitch purlwise (**01.** The Slippy One)
- purl (**03**. The Purly One)
- follow a knitting pattern containing abbreviations (**04**. The Seedy One)
- read a knitting chart (**05**. The Charted One)
- decrease by knitting two stitches together (**06**. The Mitred One)
- knit or purl a stitch through the back loop (**09**. The Twisted One)

### NEW ABBREVIATIONS

**kfb:** knit front and back

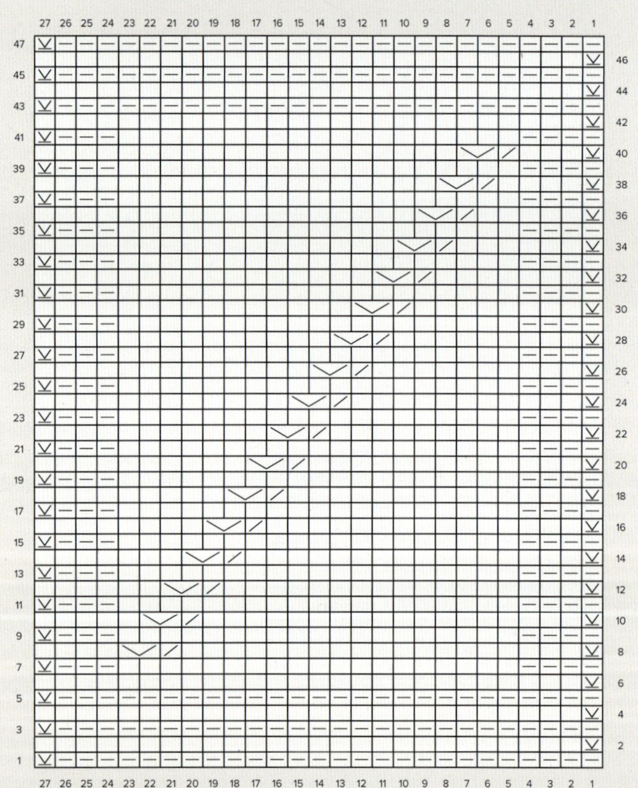

### CHART KEY

- RS: k / WS: p
- kfb
- k2tog
- RS: p / WS: k
- Sl1p

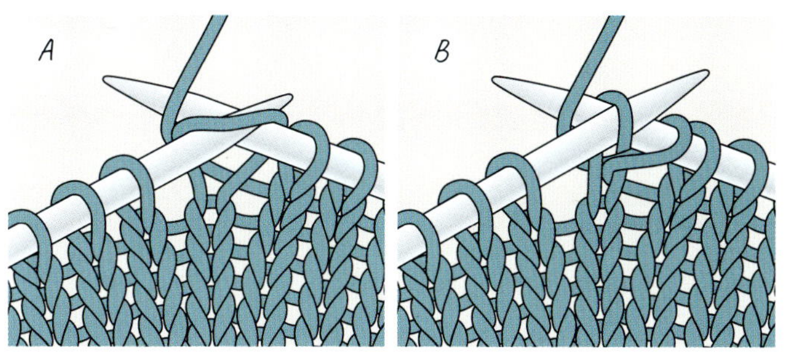

## Instructions

Cast on 27 sts.

Work according to chart as follows:

**Rows 1–6:** Sl1p, k26.
**Row 7 (WS):** Sl1p, k3, p19, k4.
**Row 8 (RS):** Sl1p, k19, k2tog, kfb, k4.

**To make a kfb:** knit a st without slipping it off the LH needle **(A)**, then knit it again through the back loop **(B)** and slip it off the LH needle.

In Row 8 you have decreased a st by knitting 2 together and you have added a st by knitting a st twice. Check that you still have 27 sts in total!

**Row 9 (WS):** Sl1p, k3, p19, k4.
**Rows 10–47:** Continue according to chart.

Cast off and weave in ends.

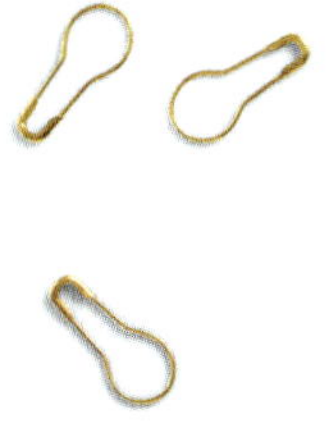

## GEEKY NOTES 

This is an easy increase and is often used in garter stitch. It is normally not used if you want invisible symmetrical increases, because the horizontal bar it creates is quite visible. In addition, its counterpart, the mirrored kfb (see **44.** The Really Nerdy One), is more complicated and not very widely known.

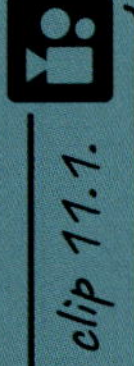

See clip 11.1.

# 11. The Convergent One

## *How to make a double decrease*

If you want to decrease from three stitches to one, you need to make a double decrease. More often than not, you will want the middle stitch to lie on top. This is called a "centred double decrease".

### YOU ALREADY KNOW HOW TO

- cast on, knit, and cast/bind off (**00**. The Basic One)
- slip the first stitch purlwise (**01.** The Slippy One)
- purl (**03**. The Purly One)
- follow a knitting pattern containing abbreviations (**04**. The Seedy One)
- read a knitting chart (**05**. The Charted One)
- decrease by knitting two stitches together (**06**. The Mitred One)
- make a yarn over (**07**. The Holey One)
- make a left-leaning decrease (**08**. The Left One)

### NEW ABBREVIATIONS

**CDD:** centred double decrease

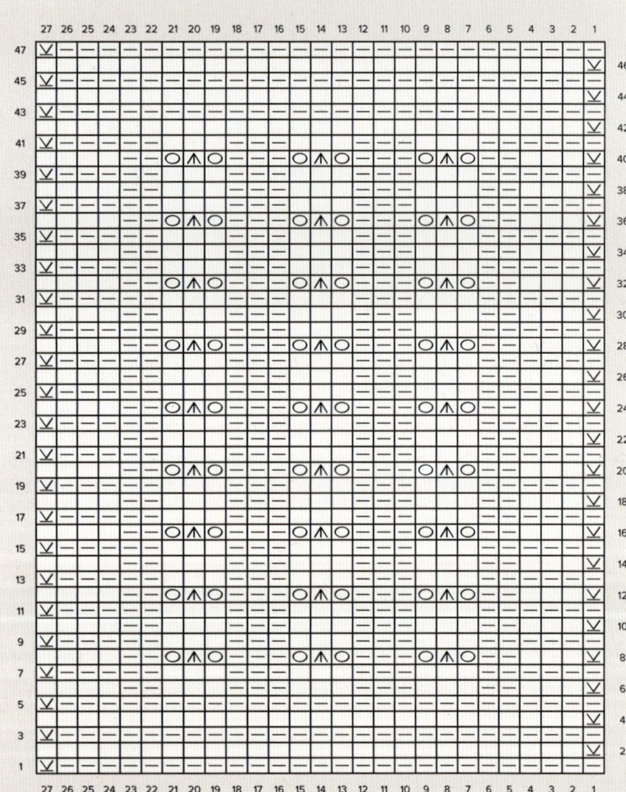

### CHART KEY

- ⋀ CDD
- ☐ RS: k / WS: p
- ⊟ RS: p / WS: k
- V Sl1p
- O YO

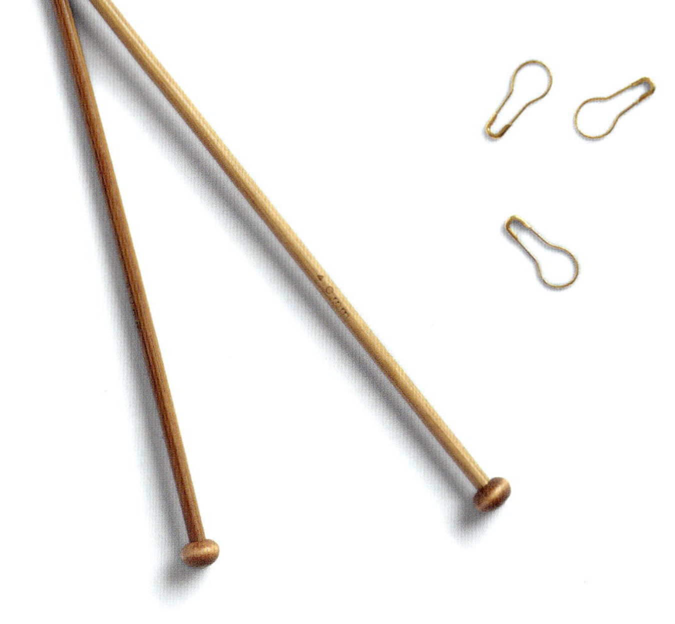

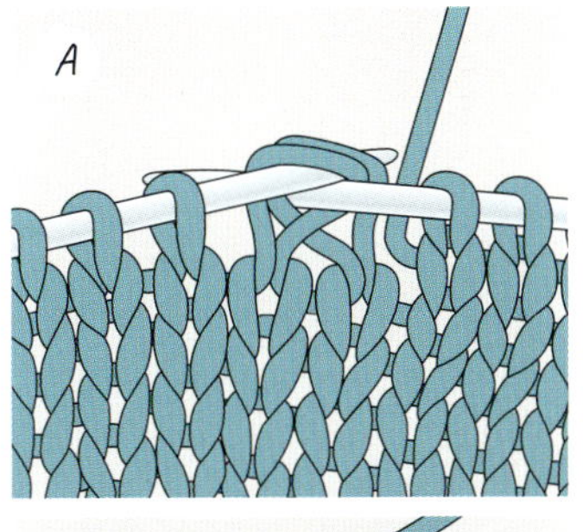


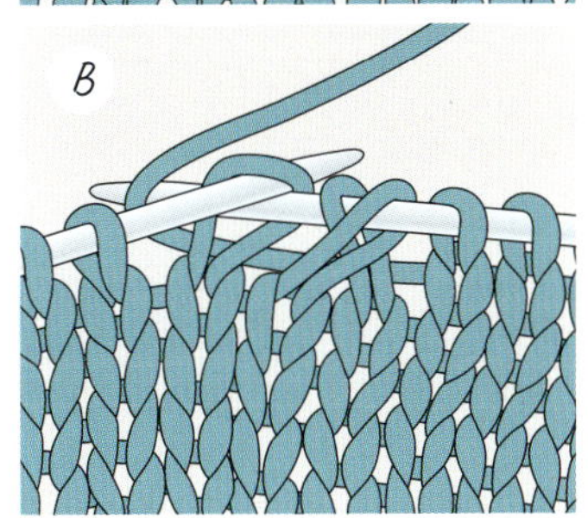


## Instructions

Cast on 27 sts.

Work according to chart as follows:

**Rows 1–5:** Sl1p, k26.
**Row 6 (RS):** Sl1p, k3, p2, [k3, p3] twice, k3, p2, k4.
**Row 7 (WS):** Sl1p, k5, [p3, k3] twice, p3, k6.
**Row 8 (RS):** Sl1p, k3, p2, [YO, CDD, YO, p3] twice, YO, CDD, YO, p2, k4.

**To make a CDD:** sl 2 sts together knitwise **(A)**, knit the next st **(B)**, pass the 2 sl sts over.

**Rows 9–47:** Continue according to chart.

Cast off and weave in ends.

## GEEKY NOTES

There are other ways of decreasing three stitches to one:

- **Sk2po:** sl the first st knitwise, k2tog, pass the slipped stitch over the k2tog
- **k3tog:** knit 3 sts together
- **SSSK:** sl 3 sts knitwise one by one, knit all 3 sl sts together through the back loops, like you do with the SSK

The first of these techniques produces a symmetrical decrease with the middle stitch underneath the two others. You will encounter this decrease in **13.** The Loopy One. The other two double decreases are right-leaning and left-leaning respectively.

See clip 12.1.

# 12. The Budding One

## *How to make a double increase*

By working the same stitch three times or more, you can make a double or multiple increase. This kind of increase is mostly used in ornamental designs.

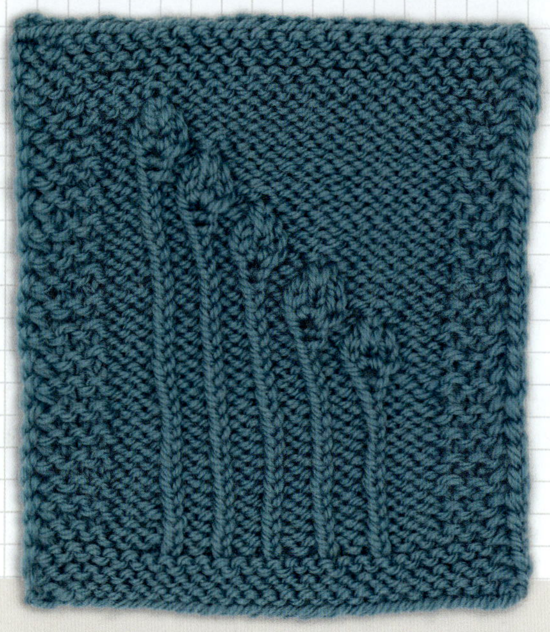

### YOU ALREADY KNOW HOW TO

- cast on, knit, and cast/bind off (**00**. The Basic One)
- slip the first stitch purlwise (**01.** The Slippy One)
- purl (**03**. The Purly One)
- follow a knitting pattern containing abbreviations (**04**. The Seedy One)
- read a knitting chart (**05**. The Charted One)
- knit or purl a stitch through the back loop (**09**. The Twisted One)
- make a double decrease (**11**. The Convergent One)

### NEW ABBREVIATIONS

**kyok:** knit, yarn over, knit into the same st

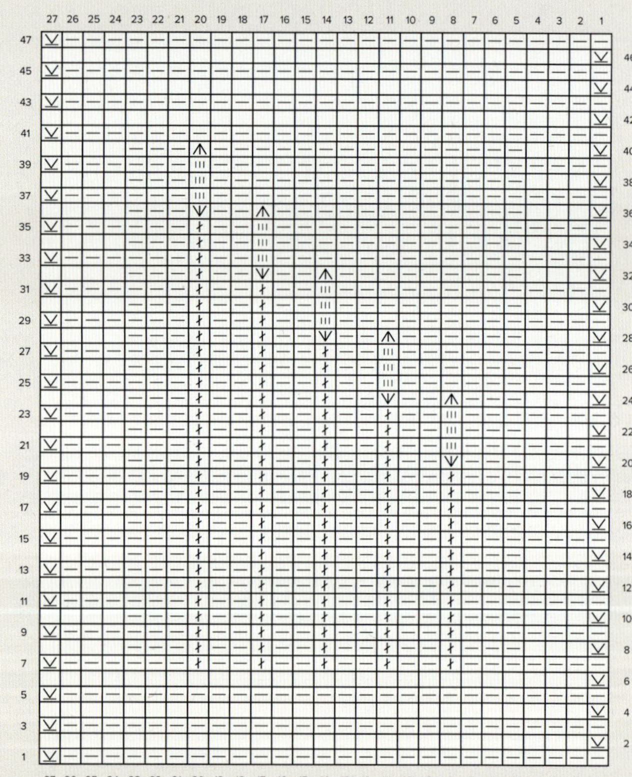

### CHART KEY

- CDD
- RS: k / WS: p
- k3
- RS: k1 tbl / WS: p1 tbl
- kyok
- RS: p / WS: k
- Sl1p

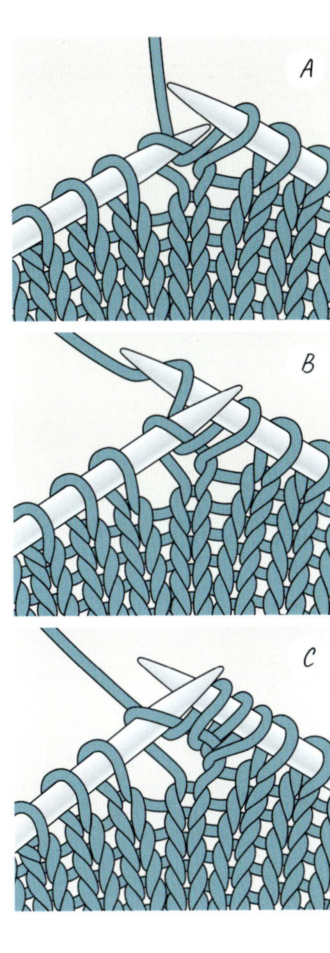


## Instructions

Cast on 27 sts.

Work according to chart as follows:

**Rows 1–6:** Sl1p, k26.
**Row 7 (WS):** Sl1p, k6, [p1 tbl, k2] 4 times, p1 tbl, k7.
**Row 8 (RS):** Sl1p, k3, p3, [k1 tbl, p2] 4 times, k1 tbl, p3, k4.
**Rows 9–18:** Repeat Rows 7 and 8 another 5 times.
**Row 19 (WS):** As Row 7.
**Row 20 (RS):** Sl1p, k3, p3, kyok, [p2, k1 tbl] 4 times, p3, k4. (29 sts)

**To make a kyok:** knit a st without slipping it off the LH needle **(A)**, make a yarn over **(B)** and knit the st again **(C)**, this time slipping it off the LH needle.

Because you made a double increase and no decreases in Row 20, you will at this point have 2 extra sts in the row, i.e., 29 sts in total.

Notice that in the chart the 3 sts of the kyok are all in a single square.

**Row 21 (WS):** Sl1p, k6, [p1 tbl, k2] 4 times, p3 (the sts of the kyok), k7.
**Row 22 (RS):** Sl1p, k3, p3, k3 (the sts of the kyok), [p2, k1 tbl] 4 times, p3, k4.
**Row 23 (WS):** As Row 21.

In Row 24, the 3 sts of the kyok are decreased to 1 with a CDD. 2 sts later there is a new kyok, so your st count remains at 29. In Row 40 you have a CDD but no increase, so you will return to 27 sts.

**Row 24 (RS):** Sl1p, k3, p3, CDD, p2, kyok, [p2, k1 tbl] 3 times, p3, k4.
**Rows 25–47:** Continue according to chart.

Cast off and weave in ends.

## GEEKY NOTES 

There are several ways to make a double increase:

- **kyok:** as shown in this square
- **kpk:** knit, then purl, and then knit the same st before slipping it off the LH needle
- **kfbf:** knit a st through the front loop, then through the back loop and then through the front loop again

The method you choose depends on the design. In this square, the increase should be symmetrical, so you could either use a kyok or a kpk. The kfbf increase is not symmetrical.

For a multiple increase, keep alternating knit stitches and yarn overs or knit and purl stitches or knitting through the front and the back loop.

**NOW YOU KNOW HOW TO**
make a double increase

See clip 13.1, 13.2, 13.3.

# 13. The Loopy One

## *How to make twisted-loop increases*

A way to avoid a hole when using the yarn-over increase is to knit the yarn over through the back loop in the next row. Alternatively, you can twist it immediately, which is what I prefer to do. In this square, loops are twisted in both directions to create symmetrical increases.

### *YOU ALREADY KNOW HOW TO*

- cast on, knit, and cast/bind off (**00**. The Basic One)
- slip the first stitch purlwise (**01.** The Slippy One)
- purl (**03**. The Purly One)
- follow a knitting pattern containing abbreviations (**04**. The Seedy One)
- read a knitting chart (**05**. The Charted One)
- decrease by knitting two stitches together (**06**. The Mitred One)
- make a yarn over (**07**. The Holey One)
- make a left-leaning decrease (**08**. The Left One)
- knit or purl a stitch through the back loop (**09**. The Twisted One)
- make a double decrease (**11**. The Convergent One)
- make a double increase (**12**. The Budding One)

### NEW ABBREVIATIONS

**LI:** left-leaning increase
**RI:** right-leaning increase

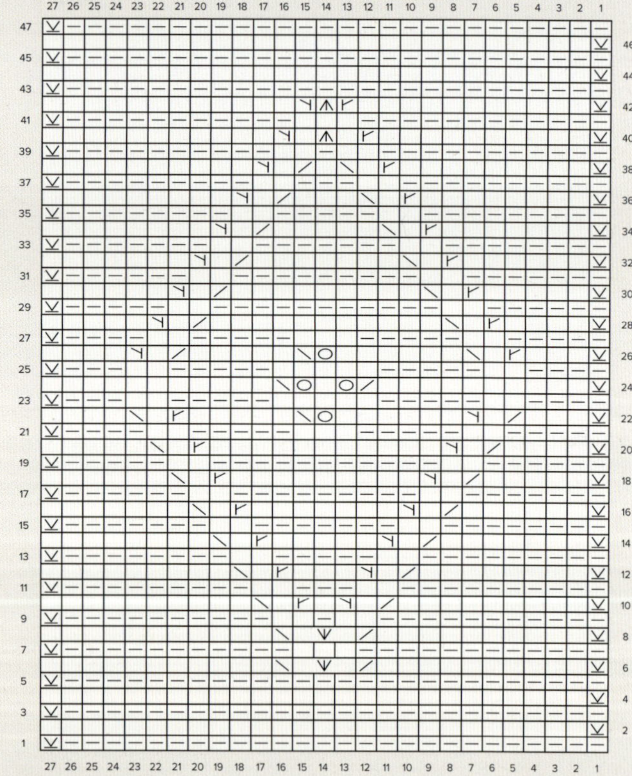

### CHART KEY

- RS: k / WS: p
- k2tog
- kyok
- LI
- RS: p / WS: k
- RI
- sk2po
- Sl1p
- SSK
- YO

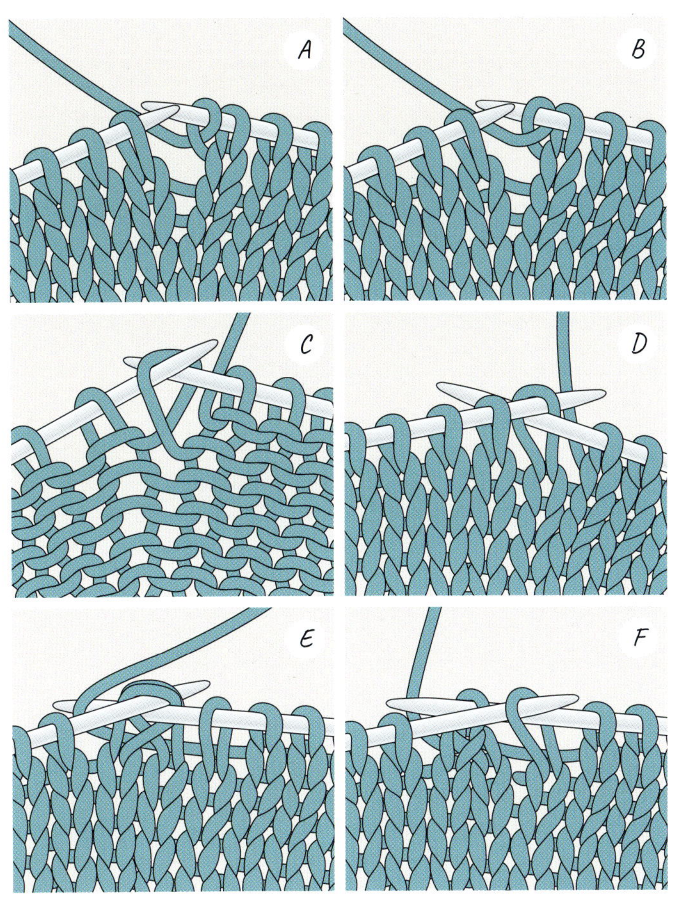


## Instructions

Cast on 27 sts.

Work according to chart as follows:

**Rows 1–5:** Sl1p, k26.
**Row 6 (RS):** Sl1p, k10, k2tog, kyok, SSK, k11.
**Row 7 (WS):** Sl1p, k11, p3, k12.
**Row 8 (RS):** Sl1p, k10, k2tog, kyok, SSK, k11.
**Row 9 (WS):** Sl1p, k10, p2, k1, p2, k11.
**Row 10 (RS):** Sl1p, k9, k2tog, k1, Ll, k1, Rl, k1, SSK, k10.

**To make an Ll:** make a loop with your working yarn on the RH needle with the front leg of the loop pointing left **(A)**. On the next row, knit this loop through the front loop, as usual.

**To make an Rl:** make a loop with your working yarn on the RH needle with the front leg of the loop pointing right **(B)**. On the next row, knit this loop through the back loop **(C)**, otherwise it will be twisted twice.

**Rows 11–47:** Continue according to chart.

On Rows 40 and 42 you will need to make a double decrease with the middle st at the bottom (as opposed to the one you learned in **11.** The Convergent One). This st is often abbreviated as sk2po.

**To work an sk2po:** sl1 **(D)**, k2tog **(E)**, pass sl st over **(F)**.

Cast off and weave in ends.

## GEEKY NOTES 

This is my favourite increase for garter stitch. It can also be used as a cast on, especially if you need to add multiple stitches at the end of a row in the middle of your project.

This increase/cast on is also known as the "backwards loop" increase/cast on. The Rl is also known as the "thumb" cast on.

make twisted-loop increases
make a double decrease with the middle stitch at the bottom

See clip 14.1, 14.2.

# **14.** The Neat One

## *How to work "make one" increases*

For neat increases in stocking stitch, you need a tighter stitch than a twisted loop. My preference is for "make one" increases, where you pick up the horizontal bar between your needles and twist it, either to the right or to the left, depending on the direction of the increase.

### YOU ALREADY KNOW HOW TO

- cast on, knit, and cast/bind off (**00**. The Basic One)
- slip the first stitch purlwise (**01.** The Slippy One)
- purl (**03**. The Purly One)
- follow a knitting pattern containing abbreviations (**04**. The Seedy One)
- read a knitting chart (**05**. The Charted One)
- decrease by knitting two stitches together (**06**. The Mitred One)
- make a yarn over (**07**. The Holey One)
- make a left-leaning decrease (**08**. The Left One)
- make a double increase (**12**. The Budding One)
- make twisted-loop increases (**13**. The Loopy One)
- make a double decrease with the middle stitch at the bottom (**13**. The Loopy One)

### NEW ABBREVIATIONS

**M1:** make one increase
**M1L:** make one left
**M1R:** make one right

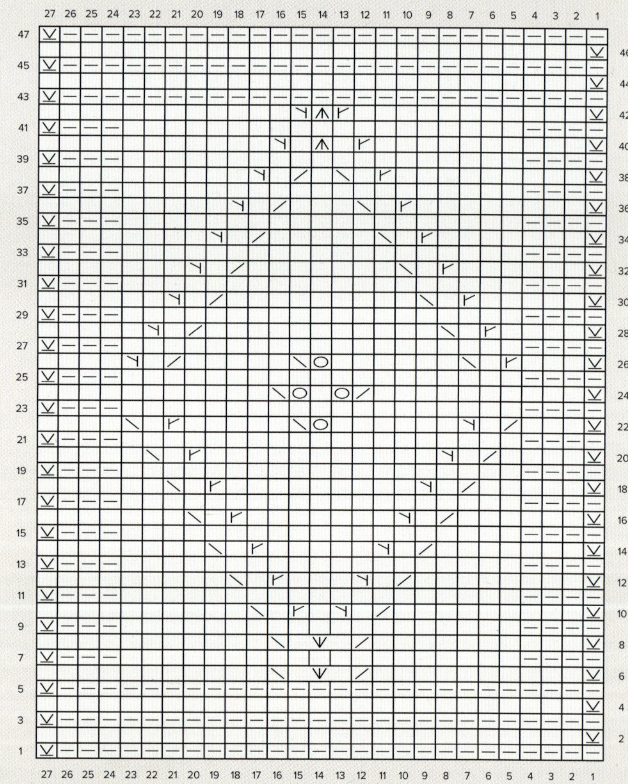


### CHART KEY

- RS: k / WS: p
- k2tog
- kyok
- M1L
- M1R
- RS: p / WS: k
- sk2po
- Sl1p
- SSK
- YO

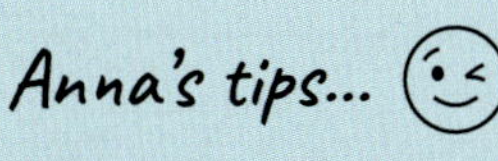


When making increases or decreases at the edges of a piece, it is best to do so after the first stitch and before the last stitch of the row, or, alternatively, after the first two and before the last two stitches.

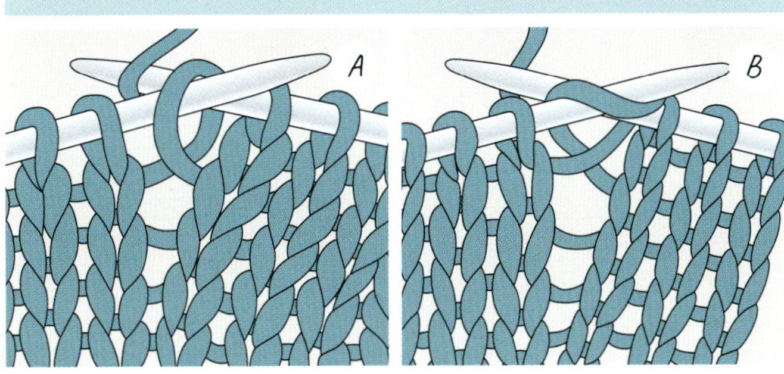


## Instructions

Cast on 27 sts.

Work according to chart as follows:

**Rows 1–5:** Sl1p, k26.
**Row 6 (RS):** Sl1p, k10, k2tog, kyok, SSK, k11.
**Row 7 (WS):** Sl1p, k3, p19, k4.
**Rows 8–9:** As Rows 6–7.
**Row 10 (RS):** Sl1p, k9, k2tog, k1, M1L, k1, M1R, k1, SSK, k10.

**To make an M1L:** pick up the horizontal bar between the needles with your RH needle from back to front, twist it to the left and knit **(A)**.

**To make an M1R:** pick up the horizontal bar between the needles with your RH needle from front to back, lift it onto your LH needle with the left leg in front and knit it through the front loop, i.e., pick the left leg **(B)**. The M1R is slightly more tricky than the M1L, because it may be difficult to get your needle in under the yarn.

The first 2 increases are made in the kyok of the previous row, so it may be harder to see which strand you need to pick up. The following rows will be easier.

**Rows 11–47:** Continue according to chart.
On Rows 40 and 42 you will need to make an sk2po (see **13.** The Loopy One).

Cast off and weave in ends.

Usually, as in this square, all shaping is done on right-side rows. Very rarely will you need to make symmetrical shaping on wrong-side (purl) rows (but you'll learn how to do this in square **15.** The Complicated One!)

NOW YOU KNOW HOW TO
work "make one" increases

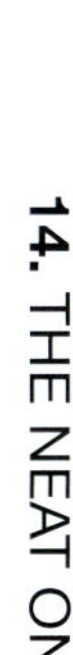

See clips 15.1, 15.2, 15.3, 15.4.

# 15. The Complicated One

## *Shaping on purl rows*

Shaping is usually done on knit rows, but occasionally you will need to make symmetrical shaping on purl rows. In this square you will learn how to make right- and left-leaning purl increases and decreases.

### YOU ALREADY KNOW HOW TO

- cast on, knit, and cast/bind off (**00.** The Basic One)
- slip the first stitch purlwise (**01.** The Slippy One)
- purl (**03.** The Purly One)
- follow a knitting pattern containing abbreviations (**04.** The Seedy One)
- read a knitting chart (**05.** The Charted One)
- decrease by knitting two stitches together (**06.** The Mitred One)
- make a yarn over (**07.** The Holey One)
- make a left-leaning decrease (**08.** The Left One)
- make a double increase (**12.** The Budding One)
- make a double decrease with the middle stitch at the bottom (**13.** The Loopy One)
- work "make one" increases (**14.** The Neat One)

### NEW ABBREVIATIONS

**M1pL:** make one purl left
**M1pR:** make one purl right
**p2tog:** purl two stitches together
**SSP:** slip, slip, purl

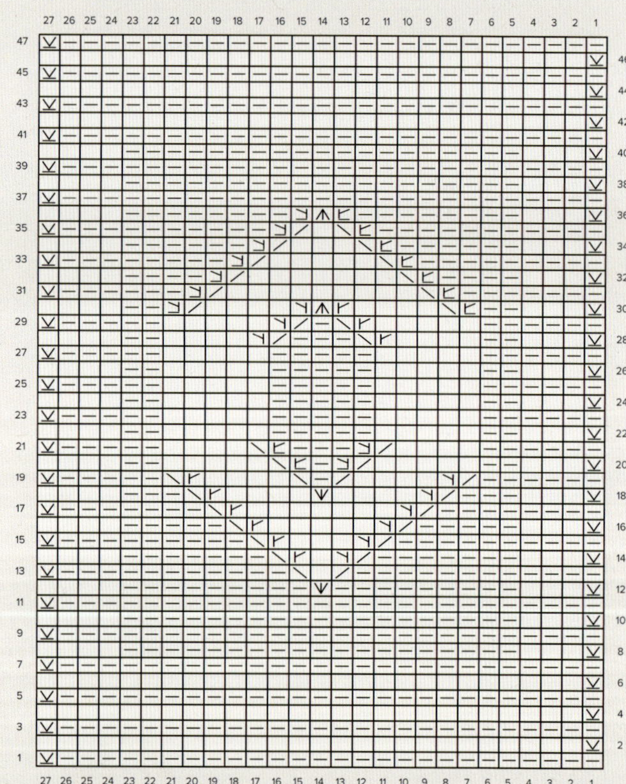

### CHART KEY

- RS: k / WS: p
- RS: k2tog / WS: p2tog
- kyok
- RS: M1R / WS: M1pR
- RS: M1L / WS: M1pL
- RS: M1pL / WS: M1L
- RS: M1pR / WS: M1R
- RS: p / WS: k
- Sl1p
- sk2po
- RS: SSK / WS: SSP

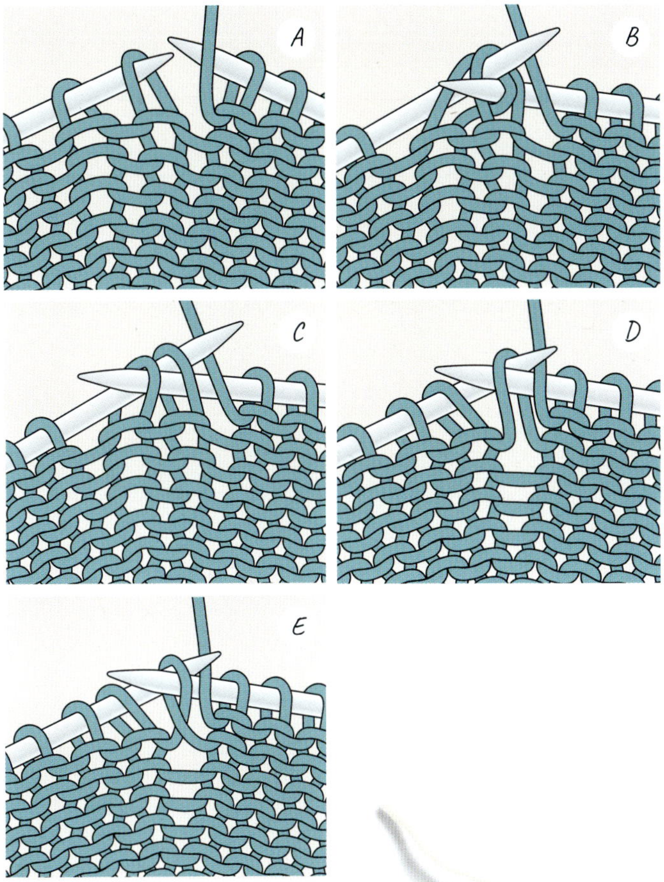

# Instructions

Cast on 27 sts.

Work according to chart as follows:

**Rows 1–7:** Sl1p, k26.
**Row 8 (RS):** Sl1p, k3, p19, k4.
**Row 9 (WS):** Sl1p, k26.
**Rows 10–11:** Repeat Rows 8–9.
**Row 12 (RS):** Sl1p, k3, p9, kyok, p9, k4. (29 sts)
**Row 13 (WS):** Sl1p, k11, SSP, p1, p2tog, k12. (27 sts)

**To make an SSP:** sl 2 sts onto the RH needle one by one, then sl them back onto the LH needle one by one with the left leg in front **(A)**, and purl these 2 sts together through the back loop **(B)**.

**To make a p2tog:** purl 2 sts together as if they were a single st **(C).**

**Row 14 (RS):** Sl1p, k3, p7, k2tog, M1L, k1, M1R, SSK, p7, k4.
**Row 15 (WS):** Sl1p, k9, SSP, M1pR, p3, M1pL, p2tog, k10.

**To make an M1pR increase:** pick up the bar between the stitches, twist it to the right and purl it **(D)**.

**To make an M1pL increase:** pick up the bar between the stitches, twist it to the left and purl it **(E)**.

**Rows 16–47:** Continue according to chart.

Cast off and weave in ends.

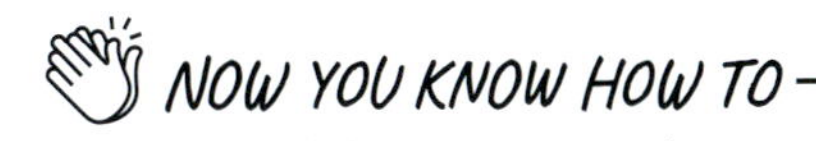


make increases and decreases on purl rows

See clip 16.1.

# 16. The Circular One

## *How to knit in the round*

A very interesting, useful technique is knitting in the round using circular and/or double-pointed needles. This way, you can knit a sweater or hat with no side seam. Another advantage is that you are always on the right side, which minimizes purling.

### YOU ALREADY KNOW HOW TO

- cast on, knit, and cast/bind off (**00**. The Basic One)
- knit horizontal stripes (**02**. The Striped One)
- purl (**03**. The Purly One)
- follow a knitting pattern containing abbreviations (**04**. The Seedy One)
- decrease by knitting two stitches together (**06**. The Mitred One)
- place and slip a marker (**06**. The Mitred One)
- make a left-leaning decrease (**08**. The Left One)

### EXTRA MATERIALS

- yarn in 2 different colours
- circular needles, 4mm (US size 6 or UK size 8), 40cm/16in long
- 5 DPNs, 4mm (US size 6 or UK size 8)
- 4 stitch markers, one of which should be different to the rest to mark the beginning of the round

### NEW ABBREVIATIONS

**rnd(s):** round(s)
**MC:** main colour
**CC:** contrast colour
**DPN(s):** double-pointed needle(s)

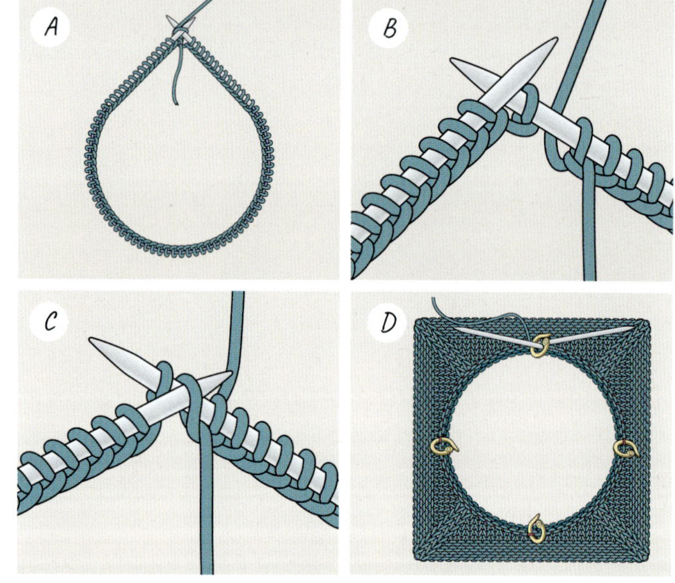

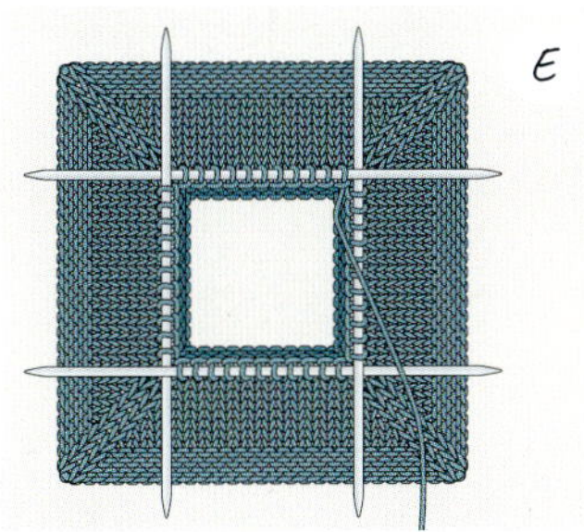


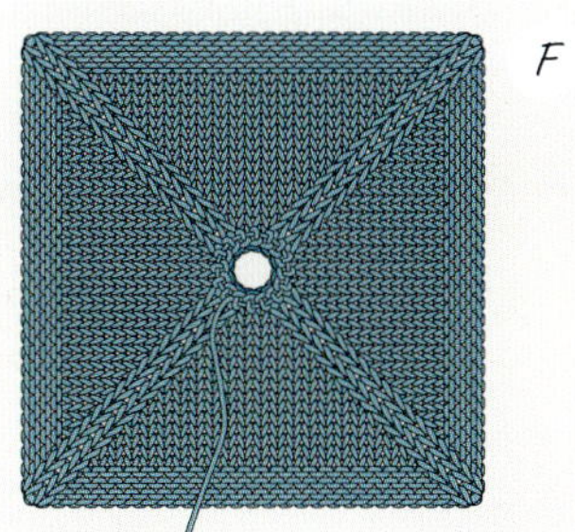


## Instructions

Note: Unless stated otherwise, whenever you encounter a stitch marker, simply slip it from the LH to the RH needle.

Using circular needles and MC, cast on 108 sts **(A)**. You will need a tail of yarn of approx 2m/80in in length.

**To get a jogless outer edge, you can cast on an extra st and pass it over the first st of the rnd as follows:** cast on an extra st, slip the first st of the rnd to the RH needle **(B)**, pass the extra st you made over it **(C)**, and return to the LH needle. Place the marker that differs from the rest to mark the beginning of the round.

Take care not to twist your sts, or you will end up with a Möbius strip.

If you did happen to twist the sts, you can still rectify the situation after the first round, when you arrive again at the beginning of the round. After that, it will be too late: the twist will show.

**Rnd 1:** Purl, PM after every 27th st.
**Rnd 2:** [SSK, k to 2 sts before marker, k2tog, SM] 4 times. (8 sts decreased)
**Rnd 3:** Purl.
**Rnd 4:** As Rnd 2. (92 sts)
**Rnd 5:** Purl.
**Rnd 6:** Knit.
**Rnds 7–8:** As Rnd 2. (76 sts)
**Rnd 9:** Knit.
**Rnds 10–11:** As Rnd 2. (60 sts)

Cut the yarn and continue with CC.

As you decrease the stitches, using circular needles will start getting difficult **(D)**. Transfer the sts to DPNs **(E)** and remove the markers as follows:

**Rnd 12:** *Take a DPN and k15, RM; repeat from * until all the sts of the round have been transferred to 4 DPNs.
**Rnd 13:** Using the fifth DPN, SSK, k11, k2tog. Using the needle that has just been freed up, work the sts on the next needle in the same way. Repeat to end of round. (52 sts)
**Rnd 14:** [SSK, k9, k2tog] 4 times. (44 sts)
**Rnd 15:** Knit.
**Rnd 16:** [SSK, k7, k2tog] 4 times. (36 sts)
**Rnd 17:** [Ssk, k5, k2tog] 4 times. (28 sts)
**Rnd 18:** Knit.
**Rnd 19:** [Ssk, k3, k2tog] 4 times. (20 sts)
**Rnd 20:** [Ssk, k1, k2tog] 4 times. (12 sts)
**Rnd 21:** Knit.

Cut the yarn leaving a 15cm/6in tail. Pass the end through the remaining sts, either with a tapestry needle, or by knitting each st and pulling the loop until the yarn passes through **(F)**. Pull the yarn to close the hole tightly and weave in all ends.

## GEEKY NOTES 

When knitting in the round, the right side of your project is always facing you. This means that knitting every round will result in stocking stitch; for garter stitch, you will have to work alternating knit and purl rounds.

When joining in the round, you get a slight jog at the beginning of the round. By casting on an extra stitch and passing it over the first stitch of the round as explained for the jogless outer edge, you can eliminate the jog.

Knitting with DPNs looks very complicated, but is in fact quite simple: you just knit as usual with two of the needles, while the others hold the stitches. You need to take care not to drop your stitches, especially if you knit very loosely or your needles are particularly heavy. You do, however, get used to it. I LOVE knitting this way, and I know I am not alone.

This square is knitted more or less in the same way as a classic hat or beanie: cast on the stitches to circular needles, work ribbing for a few cm/in, continue knitting in the round using larger (thicker) circular needles for the main body, decrease for the crown. When you are left with too few stitches for the circular needles, transfer the stitches to DPNs. Continue decreasing and, finally, cast off as above.

## Anna's tips... 

- When knitting on DPNs, if you are afraid of dropping your stitches or if you have a lot of them, you can hold them together with a rubber band **(G)**.
- When knitting with DPNs, make sure to tighten the yarn a bit more when changing needles, otherwise you may get a ladder of loose stitches at these points.
- When casting off, I like to pass the yarn through all the stitches once more before pulling tight. I make a stitch or two before weaving in the end.
- When weaving in the ends at the colour change, you can minimize the jog by going in the opposite direction from the one the yarn is coming from and sewing into the next stitch of the same colour **(H)**.
- If you find DPNs daunting, you can try the magic loop method as follows: using very long circular needles (ideally 80cm/32in long), knit half your stitches onto the circulars. Pull the right-hand needle tip so that the stitches slide onto the flexible cable, then knit the rest of the stitches. There is now a loop between the two sets of stitches **(I)**. *Turn, so the loop lies to your left. Pull the loop, sliding the front set of stitches to the left-hand needle. Pull out the right-hand needle tip so the second set of stitches is on the cable. Knit the stitches from the left-hand needle. Repeat from *.
- With the magic loop, you need to take even more care to tighten the yarn when changing needles to avoid ladders.
- Another option for knitting a small circumference project in the round is using two circulars or curved DPNs.

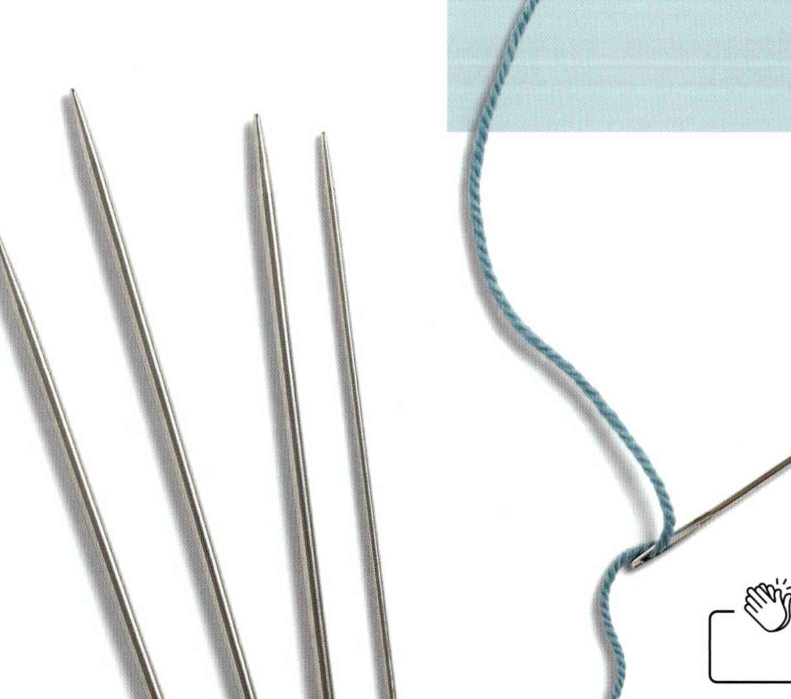

**NOW YOU KNOW HOW TO**

knit in the round

# **17.** The Jogless One

## *How to knit jogless stripes in the round*

As mentioned in **16.** The Circular One, when knitting in the round you get a jog at the beginning of the round. You will also get a jog at every colour change. If you carry the yarn from one stripe to the next, you cannot use the ends to even out the jog, so here's a neat trick you can use instead.

 *YOU ALREADY KNOW HOW TO*

- cast on, knit, and cast/bind off (**00**. The Basic One)
- knit horizontal stripes (**02**. The Striped One)
- purl (**03**. The Purly One)
- follow a knitting pattern containing abbreviations (**04**. The Seedy One)
- decrease by knitting two stitches together (**06**. The Mitred One)
- place a slip a marker (**06**. The Mitred One)
- make a yarn over (**07**. The Holey One)
- make a left-leaning decrease (**08**. The Left One)
- knit in the round (**16**. The Circular One)

### EXTRA MATERIALS

- yarn in 2 different colours
- circular needles, 4mm (US size 6 or UK size 8), 40cm/16in long
- 5 DPNs, 4mm (US size 6 or UK size 8)
- 4 stitch markers, one of which should be different to the rest to mark the beginning of the round

## Instructions

Using circular needles and MC, cast on 108 sts. Join in the round and PM to mark the beginning of the round. Take care not to twist your sts.

**Rnd 1:** Purl, PM after every 27th st.
**Rnd 2:** [SSK, k to 2 sts before marker, k2tog, SM] 4 times. (8 sts decreased)
**Rnd 3:** Purl.
**Rnd 4:** As Rnd 2. (92 sts)
**Rnd 5:** Purl.

Change to CC.

**Rnd 6:** Knit.
**Rnd 7:** As Rnd 2. (84 sts)

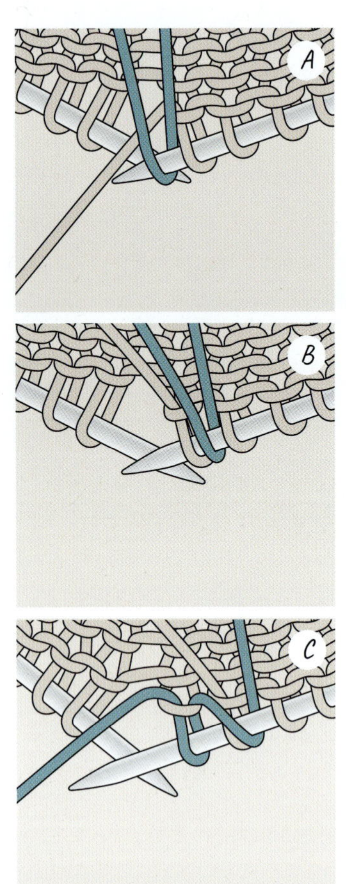


**Rnd 8:** [SSK, k to 2 sts before marker, k2tog, SM] 3 times, SSK, k to 2 sts before marker, make a YO with MC, bringing it up from behind the working yarn **(A)**, k2tog with CC **(B)**. (76 sts)

Continue with MC without twisting the yarns **(C)**.

**Rnd 9:** K to last st, k last st together with the YO.
**Rnd 10:** As Rnd 2. (68 sts)
**Rnd 11:** As Rnd 8. (60 sts)

Continue with CC.

**Rnd 12:** Knit a round, transferring the sts to DPNs and removing markers, k the last st together with the YO.
**Rnd 13:** As Rnd 2. (52 sts)
**Rnd 14:** As Rnd 8. (44 sts)

Continue with MC.

**Rnd 15:** As Rnd 9.
**Rnd 16:** As Rnd 2. (36 sts)
**Rnd 17:** As Rnd 8. (28 sts)

Continue with CC.

**Rnd 18:** As Rnd 9.
**Rnd 19:** As Rnd 2. (20 sts)
**Rnd 20:** As Rnd 8. (12 sts)

Continue with MC.

**Rnd 21:** As Rnd 9.

Break both yarns and pass the MC yarn through the remaining sts. Pull the yarn to close the hole tightly and weave in the ends.

## GEEKY NOTES 

Normally, you would make the yarn over one stitch before the colour change. Here it is made two stitches before, because the last two stitches are knitted together.

Some knitters like to slip the first stitch of the first round after the colour change to even out the jog, but this means that this stitch column will have fewer stitches than the rest, and I cannot live with that (although it does, admittedly, even out the jog). I can only encourage you to try it out, and adopt this method if it works for you!

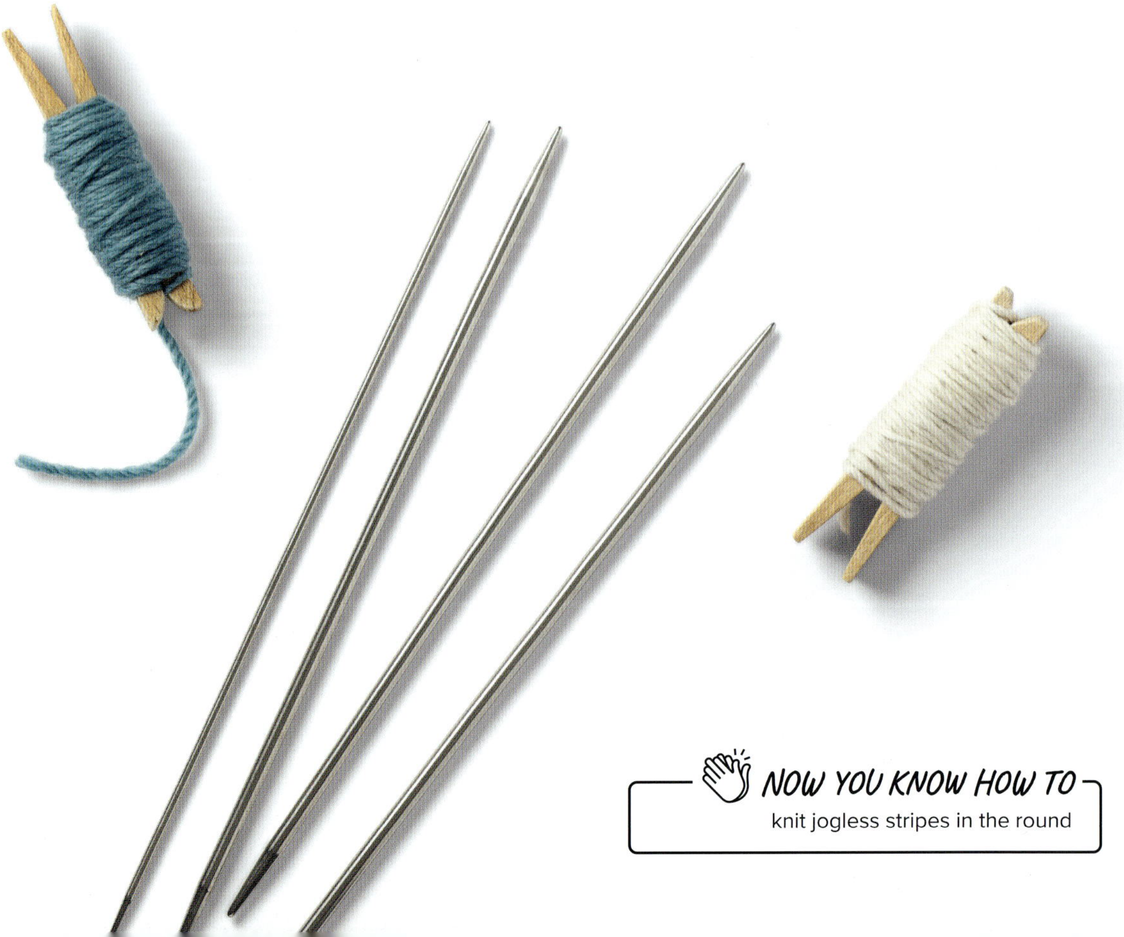

**NOW YOU KNOW HOW TO**

knit jogless stripes in the round

# 18. The Stranded One

## *How to knit stranded colourwork in the round*

With stranded knitting you can knit intricate designs in two or more colours. The colour not in use is carried along the wrong side of the work. I am going to demonstrate two ways to hold your yarns, but feel free to experiment until you find what works best for you.

See clips 18.1, 18.2.

### YOU ALREADY KNOW HOW TO

- cast on, knit, and cast/bind off (**00**. The Basic One)
- knit horizontal stripes (**02**. The Striped One)
- purl (**03**. The Purly One)
- follow a knitting pattern containing abbreviations (**04**. The Seedy One)
- read a knitting chart (**05**. The Charted One)
- decrease by knitting two stitches together (**06**. The Mitred One)
- place and slip a marker (**06**. The Mitred One)
- make a left-leaning decrease (**08**. The Left One)
- knit in the round (**16**. The Circular One)

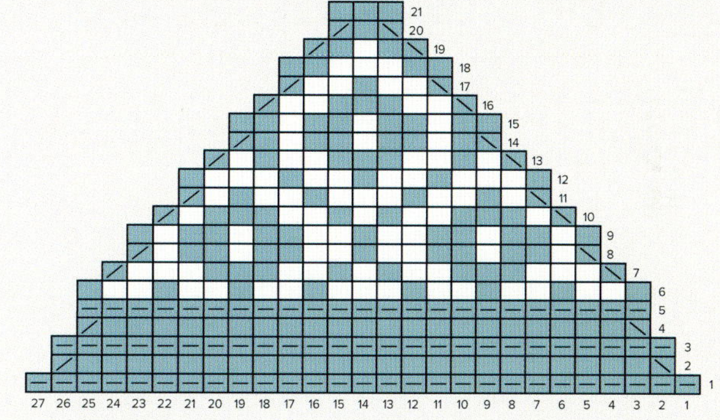


CHART KEY

- MC
- CC
- k
- k2tog
- p
- SSK

### EXTRA MATERIALS

- yarn in **2** different colours
- circular needles, **4**mm (US size **6** or UK size **8**), **40**cm/**16**in long
- **5** DPNs, **4**mm (US size **6** or UK size **8**)
- **4** stitch markers, one of which should be different to the rest to mark the beginning of the round

### NEW ABBREVIATIONS

**MC/CC:** when this follows a stitch, it denotes the colour of this stitch, e.g., "k1 MC, k2 CC" means: knit 1 stitch with the main colour, knit 2 stitches with the contrast colour.

***...**:** repeat instructions between asterisks.

# Instructions

Using circular needles and MC, cast on 108 sts. Join in the round and PM to mark the beginning of the round. Take care not to twist your sts.

**Rnd 1:** Purl, PM after every 27th st.
**Rnd 2:** [SSK, k to 2 sts before marker, k2tog, SM] 4 times. (8 sts decreased)
**Rnd 3:** Purl.
**Rnd 4:** As Rnd 2. (92 sts)
**Rnd 5:** Purl.
**Rnd 6:** Join CC. Place both yarns on your left index finger with the MC to the left **(A)**. Work Row 6 of the chart 4 times in total as follows: *[K1 MC, k2 CC] 3 times, k1 MC, k3 CC, [k1 MC, k2 CC] 3 times, k1 MC, SM.** Repeat from * to ** to end of round. Strand yarn not in use across the WS of the work.
**Rnds 7–21:** Continue according to chart, working each chart row 4 times on every round, decreasing as indicated, and transferring the sts to DPNs on Rnd 12.

When you have completed the chart, you should have 12 sts left. Cut both yarns. Pass the MC yarn through the remaining stitches.

Pull the yarn to close the hole tightly and weave in the ends.

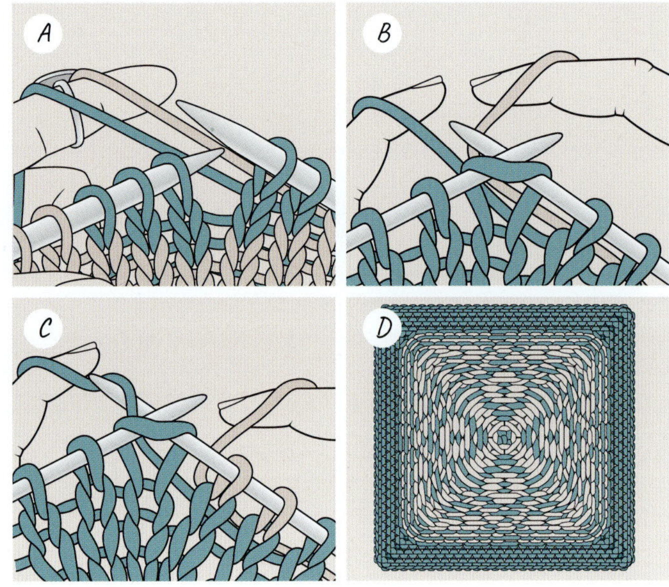


## If you are a thrower...

...you can hold both colours in your right hand, or you can try two-handed knitting: the dominant colour is held in the left hand, as in Continental knitting, and the background colour is held in the right hand, as in English style **(B, C)**.

White yarn held dominant

Blue yarn held dominant

## *Anna's tips...* 

- The strands behind the work (the "floats") need to be loose **(D)**, but not too loose! It usually takes some time for a colourwork novice to find the right tension, so be patient with yourself!
- I like to use a ring to separate the yarns on my left index finger **(A)**. I use a regular jewellery ring, but special knitting rings are also available, with small loops for the different yarn strands. Many knitters knit without any aid. I suggest you experiment to find what suits you best!
- One way of getting an even tension when working in the round is to turn your project inside out; that way your floats won't get too tight. That's not very easy to do with a square but works wonders if you're knitting socks or sleeves. It just means that you are knitting on the inside of the circle, with the floats on the outside.
- Stretch out the stitches on your right-hand needle every few stitches, especially after colour changes.
- Don't panic if the square looks like a funnel when you've finished. If you got the tension of the floats right, it will look like a normal square after washing and pressing – see Washing and Blocking
- In dense colourwork, as in this square, you can weave in the ends behind the strands on the wrong side.
- Stranded knitting often has a tighter tension than stocking stitch. If your project combines sections in stocking stitch with sections in stranded knitting, you may choose to change your needle size for the different sections accordingly.

## GEEKY NOTES 

There are many different ways of holding the yarns, when knitting colourwork. The way I learned it when I was little was to knit stitches with colour A, twist the yarns clockwise, pick up colour B and knit, twist the yarns clockwise and pick up colour A, etc. This produces a very even result, but is very labour intensive. It also means you have to untwist your balls of yarn every now and then.

A few years ago, I started knitting colourwork holding both yarns on my left index finger. Sometimes, I resort to two-handed knitting, e.g., if I'm knitting with three colours, I knit with two colours on my left index finger and one in my right hand.

I suggest you experiment a bit to see what suits you best. It is even useful to learn different techniques and choose the one best suited to the work at hand.

Unless you twist the yarns in the same direction at every colour change, as I described above, you need to be aware of colour dominance. The yarn you hold to the left produces slightly longer stitches than the yarn held to the right, making it more prominent in the pattern. In this and the following squares of this book, you should always hold the MC dominant.

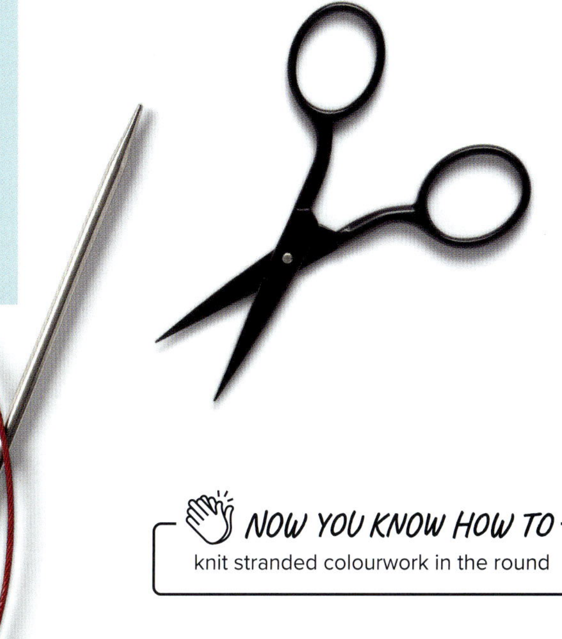

**NOW YOU KNOW HOW TO**

knit stranded colourwork in the round

See clips 19.1, 19.2, 19.3, 19.4.

# **19.** The Catchy One

## *How to catch long floats*

In stranded knitting, depending on the pattern, you sometimes get very long floats. This is not very practical: it makes it harder to keep an even tension and the floats tend to get caught in fingers and toes and other objects when wearing or using the knitted item, so it's a good idea to catch these floats onto the back side of the work.

### YOU ALREADY KNOW HOW TO

- cast on, knit, and cast/bind off (**00**. The Basic One)
- knit horizontal stripes (**02**. The Striped One)
- purl (**03**. The Purly One)
- follow a knitting pattern containing abbreviations (**04**. The Seedy One)
- read a knitting chart (**05**. The Charted One)
- decrease by knitting two stitches together (**06**. The Mitred One)
- place and slip a marker (**06**. The Mitred One)
- make a left-leaning decrease (**08**. The Left One)
- knit in the round (**16**. The Circular One)
- knit stranded colourwork in the round (**18**. The Stranded One)

### EXTRA MATERIALS

- yarn in 2 different colours
- circular needles, 4mm (US size 6 or UK size 8), 40cm/16in long
- 5 DPNs, 4mm (US size 6 or UK size 8)
- 4 stitch markers, one of which should be different to the rest to mark the beginning of the round

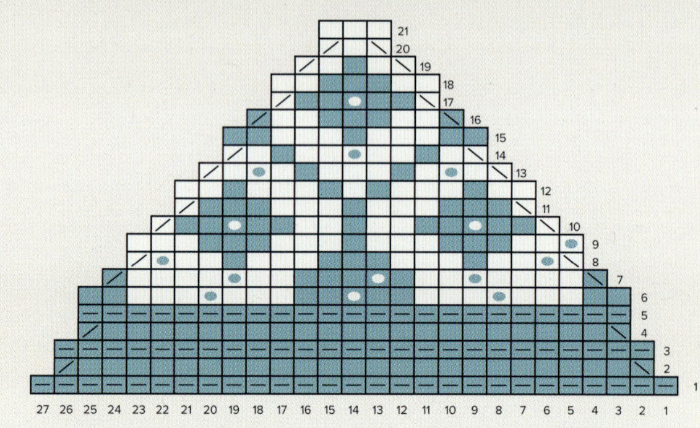


### CHART KEY

- MC
- CC
- Catch MC float on CC
- Catch CC float on MC
- k
- k2tog
- p
- SSK

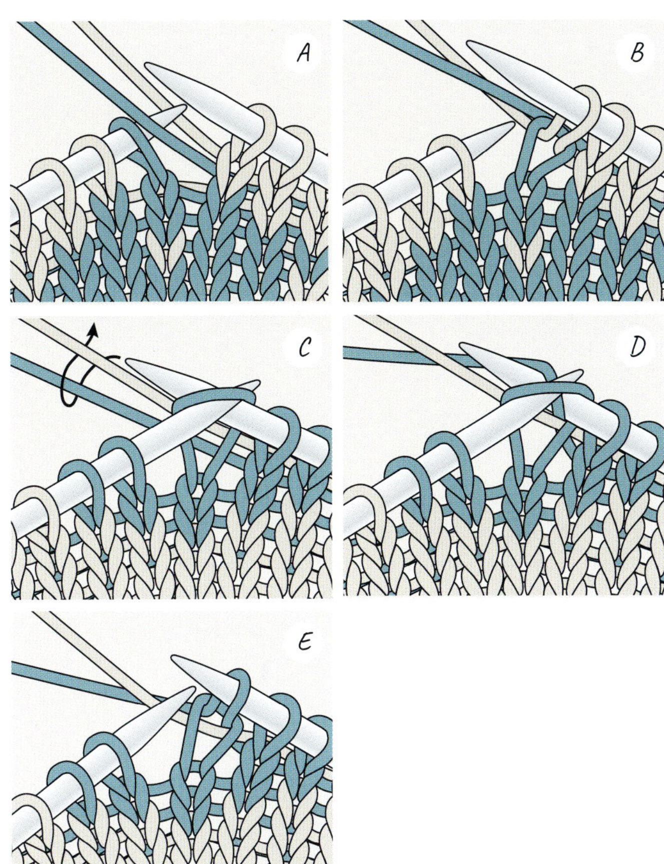


## Instructions

Note: Hold the MC dominant, i.e., to the left, throughout the square.

Using circular needles and MC, cast on 108 sts. Join in the round and PM to mark the beginning of the round. Take care not to twist your sts.

**Rnd 1:** Purl, PM after every 27th st.
**Rnd 2:** [SSK, k to 2 sts before marker, k2tog, SM] 4 times. (8 sts decreased)
**Rnd 3:** Purl.
**Rnd 4:** As Rnd 2. (92 sts)
**Rnd 5:** Purl.

On Rnd 6, you will catch the yarns.

**To catch the MC onto a CC stitch:** bring the MC yarn in front of your left-hand needle tip above the stitch you are about to knit **(A)** and knit the stitch with the CC **(B)**.

**To catch the CC onto an MC stitch:** insert the needle knitwise into the stitch, bring the needle over and around both strands of yarn **(C)** and catch the MC with the back of your needle **(D)**. Bring it back again the same way and through the loop to complete the stitch **(E)**.

Notice that to complete the catch, you also need to work the next stitch.

**Rnd 6:** Work Row 6 of the chart 4 times in total as follows: *k2 MC, k3 CC, knit the next stitch with the CC and catch the MC onto it, k3 CC, k2 MC, knit the next stitch with the MC and catch the CC onto it, k2 MC, k3 CC, knit the next stitch with the CC and catch the MC onto it, k3 CC, k2 MC, SM.** Repeat from * to ** to end of round.
**Rnds 7–21:** Continue working according to chart, working each chart row 4 times on every round, decreasing as indicated. Transfer the stitches to DPNs on Rnd 12.

When you have completed the chart, you should have 12 sts. Cut both yarns. Pass the CC yarn through the remaining stitches. Pull the yarn to close the hole tightly and weave in the ends.

## If you are a thrower...

...and knit two-handed, you will catch your floats differently.

**To catch the MC onto a CC stitch:** insert the needle knitwise into the next stitch, go underneath the MC **(F)** and knit the stitch with the CC.

**To catch the CC onto a MC stitch:** insert the needle into the stitch knitwise, wrap the CC yarn around the needle **(G)**, then wrap the MC yarn around the needle **(H)**, unwrap the CC yarn **(I)** and complete the stitch **(J)**.

### Anna's tips...

- As a general rule, I like to catch the floats every three or four stitches. If I have five or seven stitches of the same colour, I catch the yarn onto the middle one. If I have 10–14 stitches, I will catch the yarn twice or three times.
- Take care not to stack the catches, i.e., do not catch yarn onto the same stitch in consecutive rows, as the yarn will be visible on the right side of the work.
- Normally, patterns only mention that you should catch floats every x number of stitches, but do not mark the precise stitches, as I have done in this chart. I like to mark the stitches in the chart beforehand to ensure an even distribution of the catches.

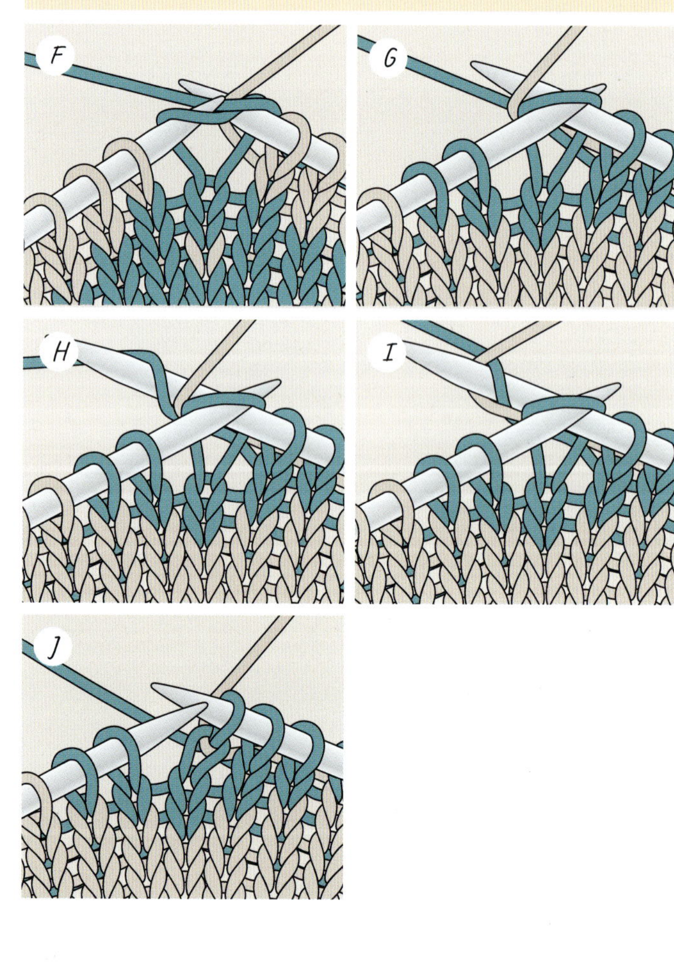


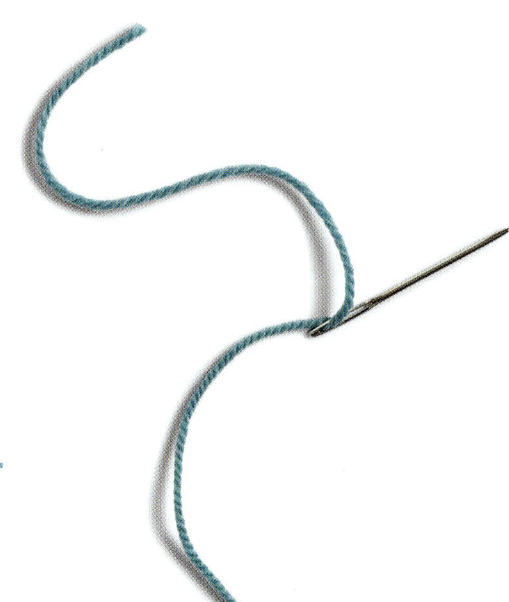

**NOW YOU KNOW HOW TO**
catch long floats

# **20.** The Square One

### *How to knit using the intarsia technique*

Intarsia is a woodwork technique for making inlaid ornaments. In knitting, it describes a technique used to knit single compact shapes using a separate ball (or bobbin) of yarn for each colour area. This way, there are no floats on the wrong side.

### YOU ALREADY KNOW HOW TO

- cast on, knit, and cast/bind off (**00**. The Basic One)
- slip the first stitch purlwise (**01**. The Slippy One)
- knit horizontal stripes (**02**. The Striped One)
- purl (**03**. The Purly One)
- follow a knitting pattern containing abbreviations (**04**. The Seedy One)
- read a knitting chart (**05**. The Charted One)

### EXTRA MATERIALS

- yarn in 2 different colours

## Instructions

For this square you will need 3 balls of yarn: 2 in the MC and 1 in the CC. In **(A)** you can see the area covered by each ball of yarn.

Using MC, cast on 27 sts.

**Rows 1–6:** Sl1p, k26.
**Row 7 (WS):** Sl1p, k3, p19, k4.
**Row 8 (RS):** Sl1p, k26.
**Rows 9–16:** Repeat Rows 7–8 another 4 times.
**Row 17 (WS):** As Row 7.
**Row 18 (RS):** Sl1p, k7, change to CC, k11, change to new MC ball of yarn, k8.
**Row 19 (WS):** Sl1p, k3, p4, change to CC, p11, change to first MC ball, p4, k4. Twist yarns at colour changes **(B,C)**.
**Rows 20–47:** Continue according to chart.

Cast off and weave in ends.

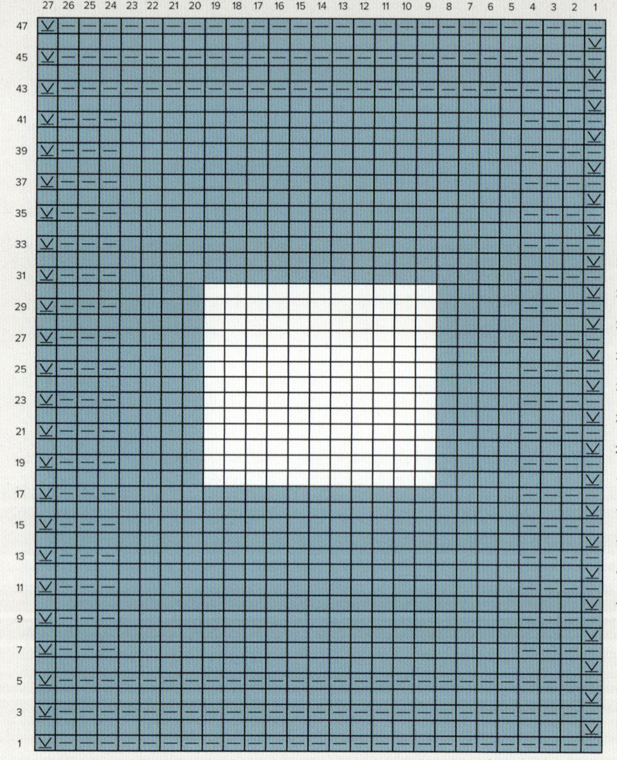

- MC
- CC
- RS: k / WS: p
- RS: pl / WS: k
- Sl1p

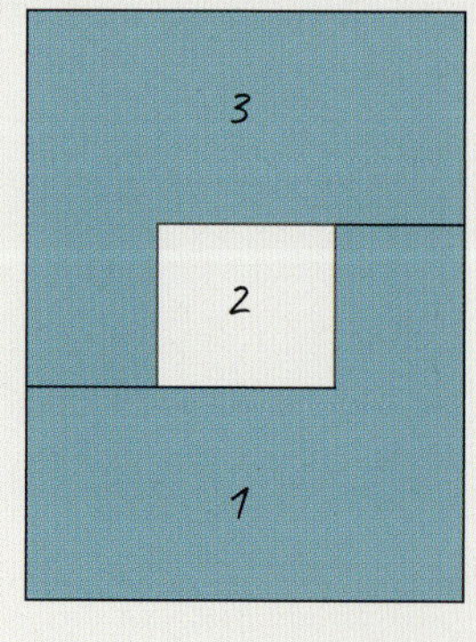

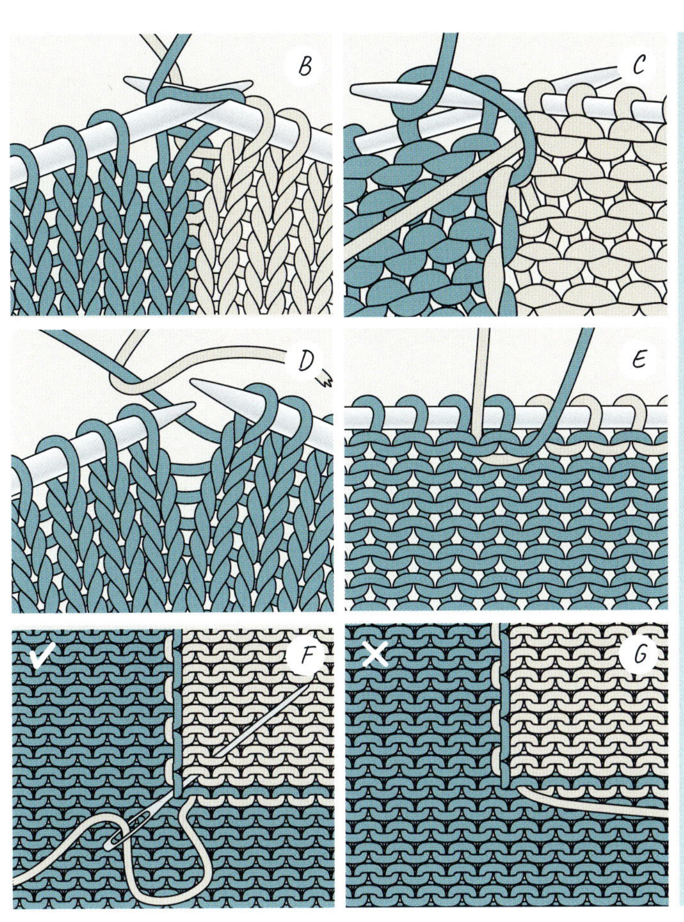


## Anna's tips...

To make your life easier, you can lock the new yarn in place one stitch before starting on a new ball/bobbin by placing it over your working yarn. This is just to stabilize the yarn while you knit the first stitch **(D, E)**. Afterwards, I pull it out from this position again before I weave in the end. You can also use this method when joining a new colour in stranded knitting.

When weaving in the ends, you want the two legs of your knit stitch to be pulled in opposite directions, so you should make sure you make the first sewing stitch in the right direction **(F)** and not "close" the two legs of the stitch **(G)**.

Back of square

**NOW YOU KNOW HOW TO**

knit using the intarsia technique

# 21. The Hearty One

## *How to make more complicated shapes in intarsia*

Matters of the heart are always complicated... This is a more advanced intarsia pattern, worked with up to five ball or bobbins per row, and with more tricky colour changes.

### YOU ALREADY KNOW HOW TO

- cast on, knit, and cast/bind off (**00**. The Basic One)
- slip the first stitch purlwise (**01**. The Slippy One)
- knit horizontal stripes (**02**. The Striped One)
- purl (**03**. The Purly One)
- follow a knitting pattern containing abbreviations (**04**. The Seedy One)
- read a knitting chart (**05**. The Charted One)
- knit using the intarsia technique (**20**. The Square One)

### EXTRA MATERIALS

- yarn in 2 different colours

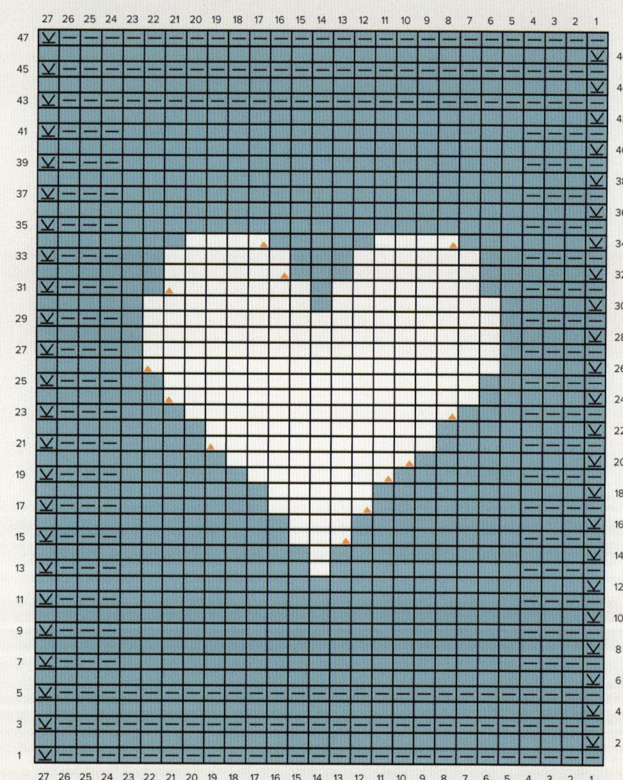


### CHART KEY

- MC
- CC
- RS: k / WS: p
- RS: p / WS: k
- Sl1p
- Twist not necessary
- Twist not necessary

4 5 2 3 1

A

## Instructions

For this square you will need 5 balls or bobbins of yarn. In **(A)** you can see the area covered by each ball of yarn.

Start by winding your balls or bobbins:

- Ball 1 will be your main ball of MC yarn.
- Ball 2 will be your main ball of CC yarn.
- Ball 3: make a ball/bobbin with 5m of MC yarn
- Ball 4: make a ball/bobbin with 1m of CC yarn.
- Ball 5: make a ball/bobbin with 1m of MC yarn.

Using MC, cast on 27 sts.

**Rows 1–6:** Sl1p, k26.
**Row 7 (WS):** Sl1p, k3, p19, k4.
**Row 8 (RS):** Sl1p, k26.
**Rows 9–12:** Repeat Rows 7–8 twice more.

On Rows 13–19 you will be working with balls 1, 2 and 3.

**Row 13 (WS):** Sl1p, k3, p9, with ball 2 (CC) p1, with ball 3 (MC) p9, k4.
**Row 14 (RS):** Sl1p, k12, with ball 2 (CC) k1, with ball 1 (MC) k13.

These first 2 rows are particularly fiddly. Make sure you knit on with the right ball of yarn – and not with the yarn end!

**Rows 15–47:** Continue according to chart.

Technically, it's not strictly necessary to twist the yarns whenever you have a left slant (seen from your point of view, while knitting), but no harm done if you do. The colour changes where it is not strictly necessary to twist the yarns are marked with an orange triangle in the chart. Whatever you choose to do, though, be consistent throughout the square!

On Rows 30–34 you will be working with all 5 balls/bobbins.

Cast off and weave in ends.

### GEEKY NOTES

It is, of course, possible to combine intarsia with stranded knitting, e.g., on Rows 30–34 you could strand the CC behind the MC for the central stitches, and thus only work with four balls of yarn instead of five.

make more complicated shapes in intarsia

See clips 22.1, 22.2.

# 22. The Flat One

## *How to knit stranded colourwork on two needles*

Stranded knitting can also be worked flat on two straight needles. On wrong side rows you will need to pass the strands in front of your work. The challenge here is to get the edge stitches neat. Here's a trick to achieve that.

### YOU ALREADY KNOW HOW TO

- cast on, knit, and cast/bind off (**00**. The Basic One)
- slip the first stitch purlwise (**01**. The Slippy One)
- knit horizontal stripes (**02**. The Striped One)
- purl (**03**. The Purly One)
- follow a knitting pattern containing abbreviations (**04**. The Seedy One)
- read a knitting chart (**05**. The Charted One)
- make a yarn over (**07**. The Holey One)
- make increases and decreases on purl rows (**15**. The Complicated One)
- knit jogless stripes in the round (**17**. The Jogless One)
- knit stranded colourwork in the round (**18**. The Stranded One)

### EXTRA MATERIALS

- yarn in 2 different colours

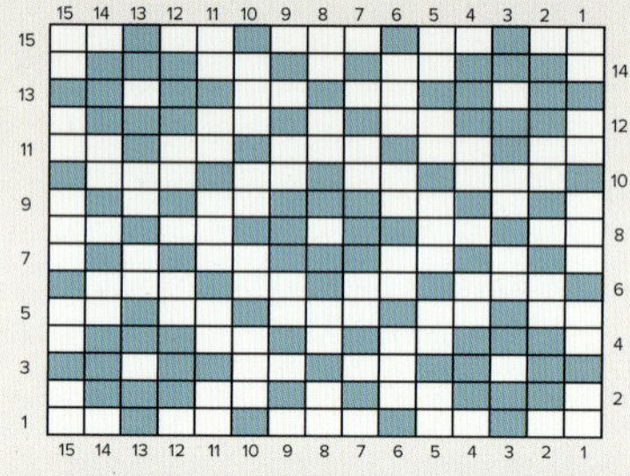


CHART KEY

- MC
- CC
- RS: k / WS: p

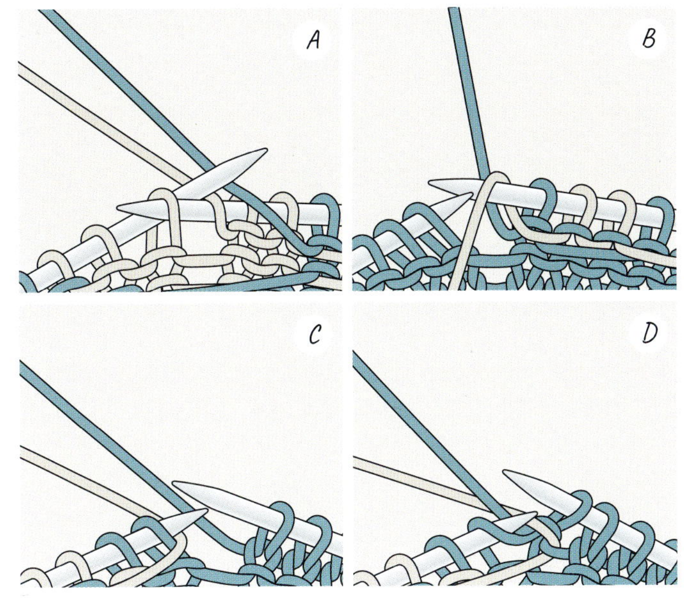


## Instructions

Using MC, cast on 27 sts.

**Rows 1–16:** Sl1p, k26.

Begin colourwork on Row 17, and hold MC dominant throughout. If you knit with both colours in your left hand, you should hold the dominant colour to the right on WS rows and to the left on RS rows. Go behind both strands before you insert the needle into the st **(A)**. Always carry the unused strand of yarn across the WS, i.e., in front of the work on WS rows and at the back on RS rows.

**Row 17 (WS):** Sl1p, k4, p1 MC, continue with both colours, placing the MC to the right on your left index finger and leaving the CC yarn end hanging in front of the work (on the WS) and work Row 1 of the chart over the next 15 sts as follows: [p2 CC, p1 MC] twice, p3 CC, [p1 MC, p2 CC] twice (you have now completed Row 1 of the chart), p1 MC, make a reverse YO with the CC, i.e., bring the yarn over the RH needle from back to front and leave the CC hanging in front (on the WS **(B)**), k5 MC.

**Row 18 (RS):** Sl1p, k4 MC and, using MC, knit next st together with the YO, pull CC yarn tight to make sure it isn't visible on the right side, holding MC yarn to the left work Row 2 of the chart, leave CC hanging on the WS, k6 MC.

**Row 19 (WS):** Sl1p, k4 MC, place the yarns on your index finger with the MC to the right **(C)** and, using the MC, purl the next st together with the CC strand **(D)**, pull the CC yarn tight to make sure it isn't visible on the RS, work Row 3 of the chart, p1 MC, make a reverse YO with the CC and leave the yarn hanging in front, k5 MC.

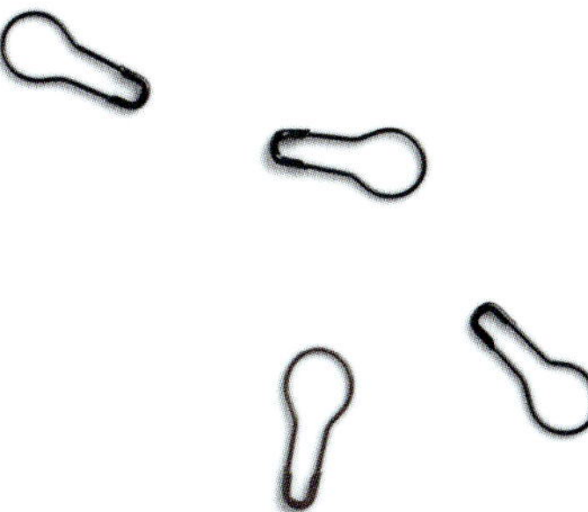

**Rows 20–30:** Continue according to chart, working a garter-st border on either side of the chart sts as established in Rows 18-19, until you have completed Row 14 of the chart.
**Row 31 (WS):** Sl1p, k4 MC, using MC purl the next st together with the CC strand, work Row 15 of the chart, bring CC to front, p1 MC, k5 MC. Break CC and continue with MC.
**Rows 32–47:** Sl1p, k26.

Cast off and weave in ends.

## If you are a thrower...

Catch the CC on WS rows as follows: Sl1p, k4 MC, place CC yarn over the MC yarn **(E)** and purl the next st **(F)**. Continue with colourwork.
Regarding colour dominance: if you knit with both colours in the right hand, you should swap the position of the yarns on the purl side rows.
If you knit with one colour in each hand, you should not change the position of the yarns **(G, H)**.

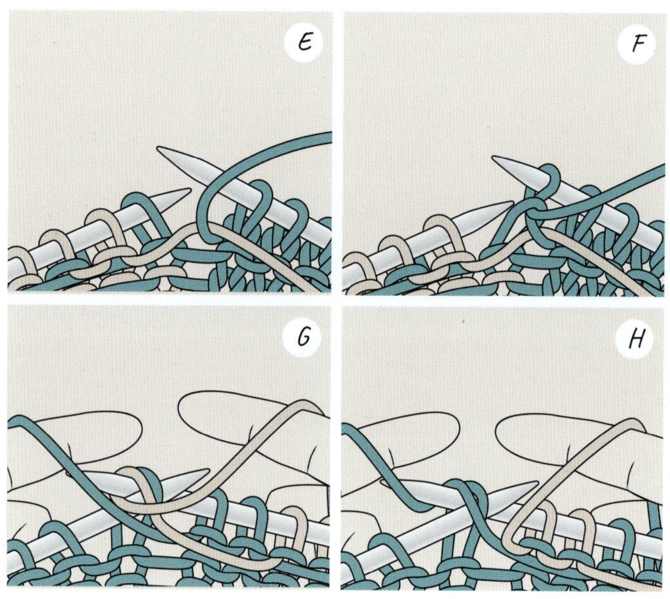

## GEEKY NOTES

Stranded knitting is undoubtedly easier when worked in the round. Many people (including yours truly) even prefer to work cardigans in the round and subsequently cut them up, making a "steek".

**NOW YOU KNOW HOW TO**
knit stranded colourwork on two needles

# 23. The Difficult One

## *How to catch floats on wrong-side rows*

Catching long floats on wrong-side rows is probably not something you'll be doing very often, but for the sake of completeness I have included it here.

### YOU ALREADY KNOW HOW TO

- cast on, knit, and cast/bind off (**00**. The Basic One)
- slip the first stitch purlwise (**01**. The Slippy One)
- knit horizontal stripes (**02**. The Striped One)
- purl (**03**. The Purly One)
- follow a knitting pattern containing abbreviations (**04**. The Seedy One)
- read a knitting chart (**05**. The Charted One)
- make a yarn over (**07**. The Holey One)
- make increases and decreases on purl rows (**15**. The Complicated One)
- knit jogless stripes in the round (**17**. The Jogless One)
- knit stranded colourwork in the round (**18**. The Stranded One)
- catch long floats (**19**. The Catchy One)
- knit stranded colourwork on two needles (**22**. The Flat One)

### EXTRA MATERIALS

- yarn in 2 different colours

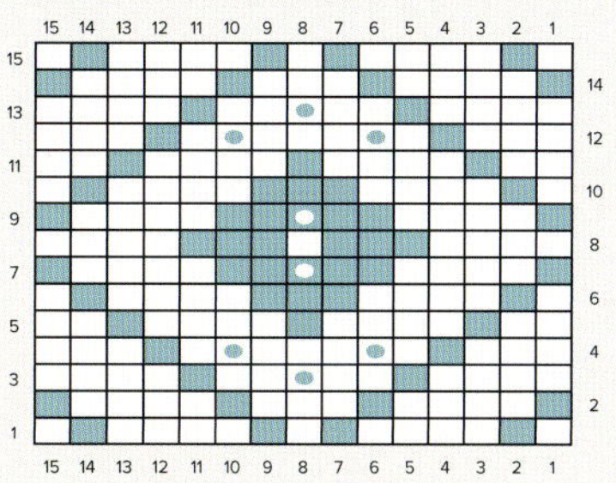

### CHART KEY

- MC
- CC
- RS: k / WS: p
- Catch MC float on CC
- Catch CC float on MC

## Instructions

Using MC, cast on 27 sts.

**Rows 1–16:** Sl1p, k26.

Begin colourwork on Row 17, and hold MC dominant throughout.

**Row 17 (WS):** Sl1p, k4, p1 MC, continue with both colours, placing the MC to the right on your left index finger and leaving the CC yarn end hanging in front of the work, work Row 1 of the chart over the next 15 sts as follows: p1 CC, p1 MC, p4 CC, p1 MC, p1 CC, p1 MC, p4 CC, p1 MC, p1 CC (you have now completed Row 1 of the chart), p1 MC, make a reverse YO with the CC and leave it hanging in front (on the WS), k5 MC.

**Row 18 (RS):** Sl1p, k4 MC and, using MC, knit next st together with the YO, pull CC yarn tight to make sure it isn't visible on the RS, holding MC yarn to the left work Row 2 of the chart, leave CC hanging on the WS, k6 MC.

On Row 19 (Row 3 of the chart) you will need to catch the MC onto a CC st.

**To catch the MC onto a CC st:** insert the needle purlwise into the st **(A)**, bring the needle over and behind both strands of yarn **(B)** and catch the CC with the back of your needle **(C)**. Bring it down in front and back through the loop to complete the st the same way you would normally complete a purl st **(D)**. Remember that the catch is complete, only after you've worked the next st.

**Row 19 (WS):** Sl1p, k4 MC, place the yarns on your index finger with the MC to the right and, using the MC, purl the next st together with the CC strand, pull the CC yarn tight to make sure it isn't visible on the RS, work Row 3 of the chart, p1 MC, make a reverse YO with the CC and leave it hanging in front, k5 MC.

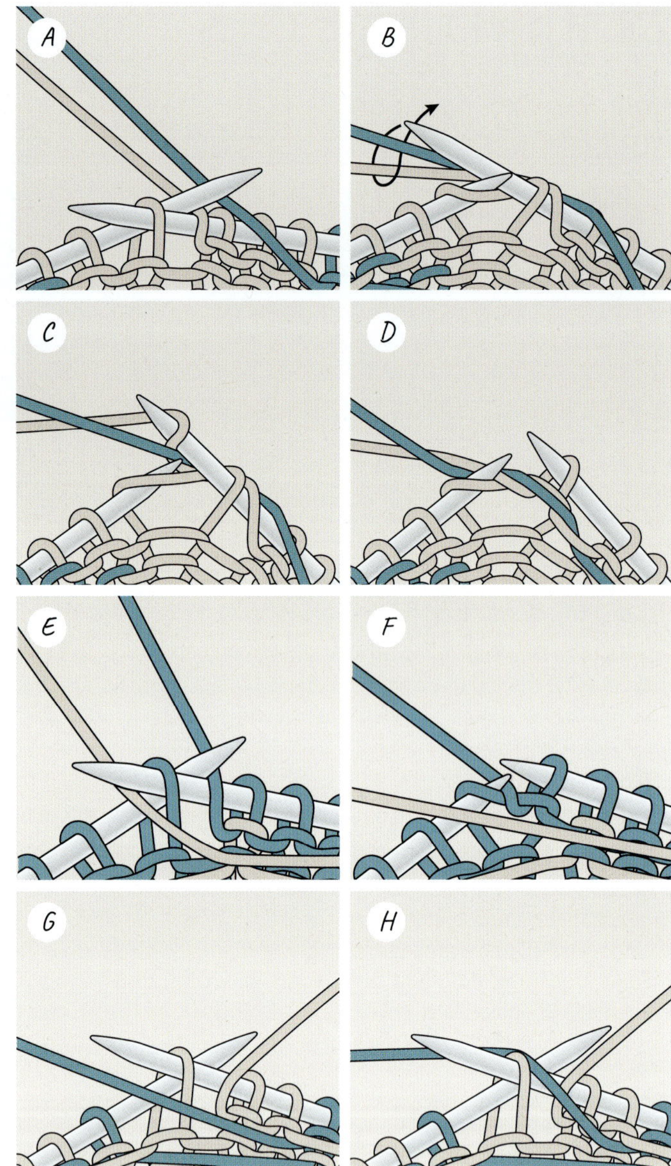

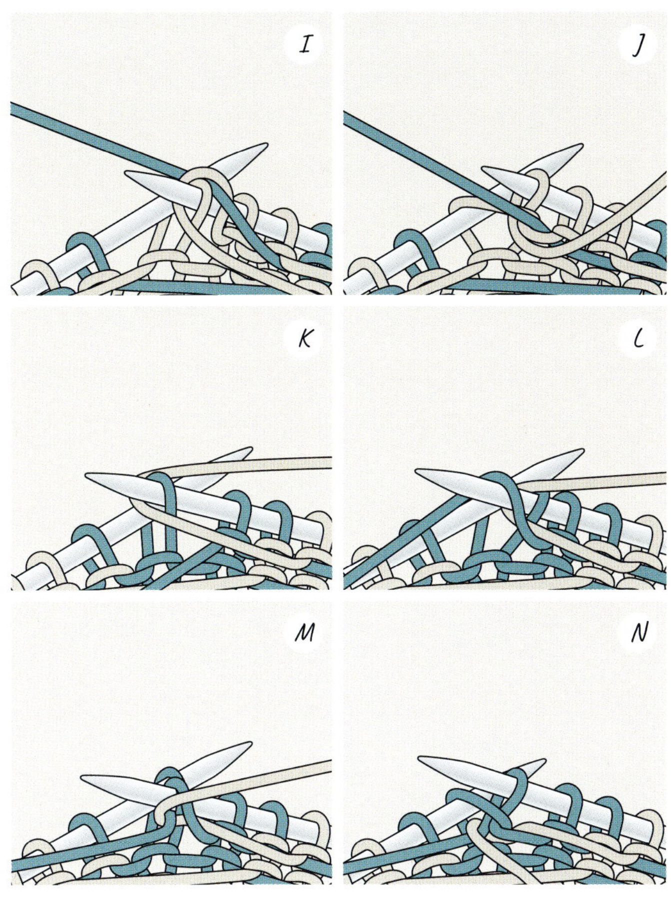


**Rows 20–30:** Continue according to chart, working a garter-st border on either side of the chart sts as established in Rows 18-19, until you have completed Row 14 of the chart. On Row 23 (Row 7 of the chart) you will need to catch the CC onto a MC st.

**To catch the CC onto a MC st:** hold the CC down in front of your LH needle **(E)** and purl the st with the MC **(F)**. Let go of the CC to return to normal position before you work the next st.

**Row 31 (WS):** Sl1p, k4 MC, using the MC, purl the next st together with the CC strand, work Row 15 of the chart, bring CC to front, p1 MC, k5 MC.

Break CC and continue with MC.

**Rows 32–47:** Sl1p, k26.

Cast off and weave in ends.

## If you are a thrower...

...and knit two-handed, you will catch your floats differently.

**To catch the MC onto a CC st:** insert the needle purlwise into the st **(G)** and bring the MC over the RH needle tip **(H)**. Wrap the CC around the needle to purl as normal **(I)** and complete the st **(J)**.

**To catch the CC onto an MC st:** insert the RH needle purlwise into the st and wrap the CC yarn around the needle the "wrong" way, i.e., from underneath the needle **(K)**. Wrap the MC around the needle **(L)**. Unwrap the CC yarn **(M)** and complete the st **(N)**.

**NOW YOU KNOW HOW TO**

catch floats on wrong-side rows

See clip 24.1.

# 24. The Mosaic One

## *How to work the mosaic technique*

Mosaic knitting uses slipped stitches to form colourwork patterns. Unlike stranded knitting, you only work with one colour in every row. Slip stitches with the yarn in the back on right-side rows and with the yarn in front on wrong-side rows.

### *YOU ALREADY KNOW HOW TO*

- cast on, knit, and cast/bind off (**00**. The Basic One)
- slip the first stitch purlwise (**01**. The Slippy One)
- knit horizontal stripes (**02**. The Striped One)
- purl (**03**. The Purly One)
- follow a knitting pattern containing abbreviations (**04**. The Seedy One)
- read a knitting chart (**05**. The Charted One)

### EXTRA MATERIALS

- yarn in 2 different colours

### NEW ABBREVIATIONS

**wyib:** with the yarn in the back
**wyif:** with the yarn in the front

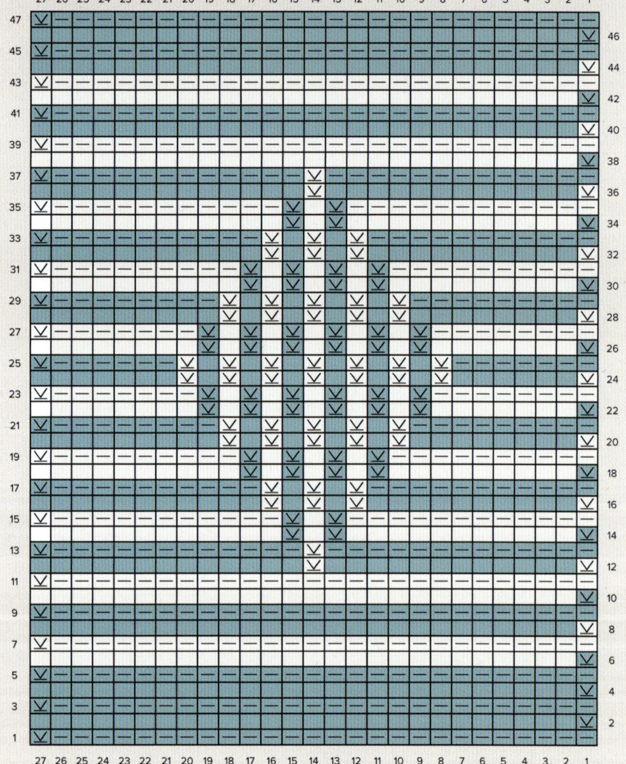

### CHART KEY

- MC
- CC
- RS: k / WS: p
- RS: p / WS: k
- RS: Sl1p wyib / WS: Sl1p wyif

## *Anna's tips...*

You may remember that I like to weave in the very first end in advance. When possible, I also like to do that when I join a new colour.

Sew the yarn end of the new colour into the yarn **(C)**, making a loop **(D)**. Insert the RH needle into a stitch and, instead of wrapping the yarn around the needle, insert the needle into the loop **(E)**. Pull the loop through the stitch **(F)**. This is your first stitch in the new colour. For these squares, this is done on the second stitch of the row, since the first one is slipped. If the first stitch is knitted, the colour change occurs on the first stitch.

Why, oh, why haven't I mentioned this before, so you didn't have to weave in all the loose ends in the colourwork and intarsia squares? The truth is that this technique works really well when you have to change colour at the beginning of the row, as in this square, but it doesn't work as well when you have a colour change in the middle of a row, as in stranded knitting or intarsia. You may remember that in intarsia and in colourwork you want to take care not to "close" the first or last stitch when weaving in the end. This technique does precisely that. The two legs of the selvedge stitch, however, both point in the same direction, so there's no harm done if you weave the end into the working yarn.

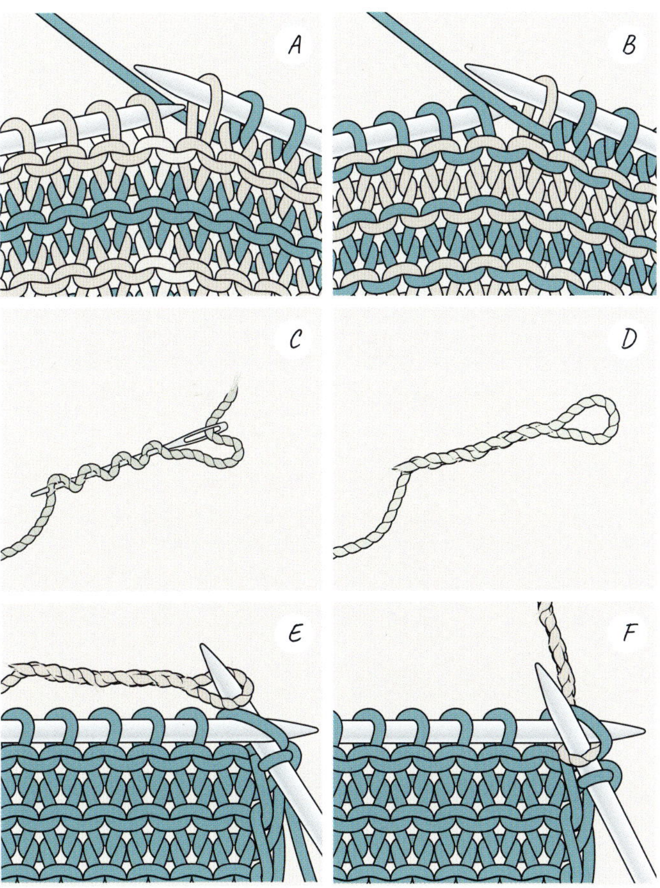


## Instructions

Using MC, cast on 27 sts.

**Rows 1–5:** Sl1p, k26.
**Rows 6 and 7:** With CC, sl1p, k26.
**Rows 8 and 9:** With MC, sl1p, k26.
**Rows 10 and 11:** With CC, sl1p, k26.
**Row 12 (RS):** With MC, sl1p, k12, sl1p wyib, k13.

**To sl a st purlwise wyib:** insert the RH needle into the st from right to left and transfer it to the LH needle. The working yarn lies behind the st **(A)**.

**Row 13 (WS):** Sl1p, k12, sl1p wyif, k13.

**To sl a st purlwise wyif:** insert the RH needle into the st from right to left, passing behind the working yarn as if to purl it. Transfer the st to the LH needle and bring the working yarn into position to work the next st. The working yarn lies in front of the sl st. Notice that the motion is very much the same as slipping the selvedge st purlwise **(B)**.

**Rows 14–47:** Continue according to chart, changing colour every 2 rows.

Cast off and weave in ends.

See clips 25.1, 25.2

# 25. The Braided One

## How to make a Latvian Braid

You might have noticed that there is a certain kind of beauty in the regular floats on the wrong side of stranded knitting. Latvian braids bring these floats onto the right side. However, to achieve the braid effect, the yarns need to be twisted at every colour change.

 YOU ALREADY KNOW HOW TO

- cast on, knit, and cast/bind off (**00**. The Basic One)
- slip the first stitch purlwise (**01**. The Slippy One)
- knit horizontal stripes (**02**. The Striped One)
- purl (**03**. The Purly One)
- follow a knitting pattern containing abbreviations (**04**. The Seedy One)
- knit stranded colourwork in the round (**18**. The Stranded One)
- knit stranded colourwork on two needles (**22**. The Flat One)

EXTRA MATERIALS

- approx 1.3m/50in of contrast colour yarn for each braid. You can choose to make all the braids in the same colour or in different colours.

## Instructions

Using MC, cast on 27 sts.

**Rows 1–5:** Sl1p, k26.

Row 6 is the set-up row for the braid.

**Row 6 (RS):** Sl1p, k3. Continue with MC and CC and stranding yarn not in use loosely across WS, k1 CC, [k1 MC, k1 CC] 9 times, bring CC yarn to the front and leave it there, k4 MC.

This row will not be visible once the braid is finished, so you can hold either colour dominant, but be consistent throughout the row.

**Row 7 (WS):** Sl1p, k3, start braid as follows: k1 CC, [stranding yarn not in use across RS, i.e., behind the work from your point of view, pick up MC from underneath CC yarn **(A)** and k1 with MC, pick up CC from underneath MC yarn and k1 with CC] 9 times, leave the CC hanging on the RS, k4 MC.

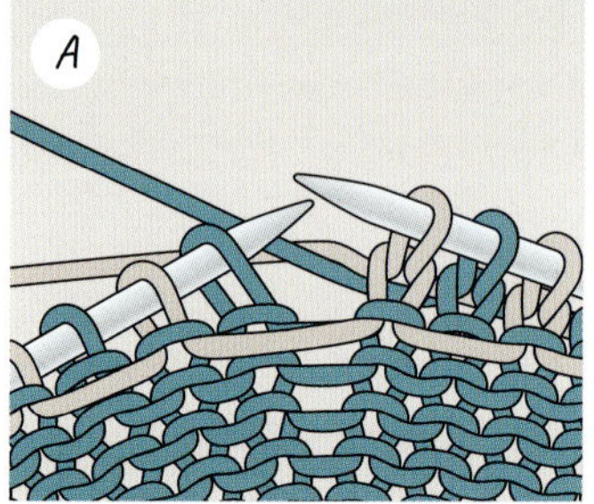


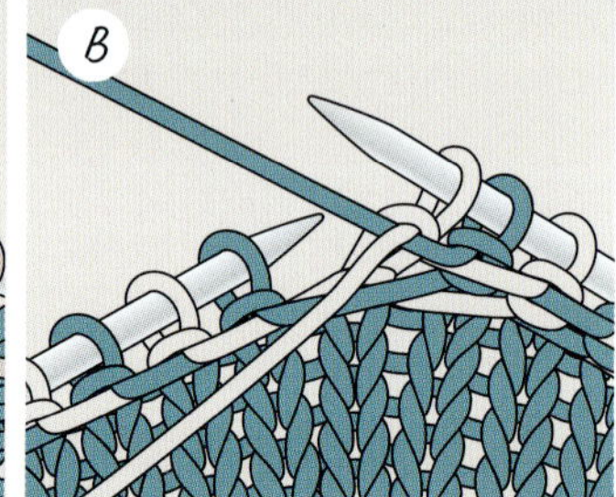

Your yarns are now twisted. Do not untwist them!!! They will untwist themselves on the next row.

**Row 8:** (RS) Sl1p, k3 MC, bring MC to front, p1 CC, [hold CC in front and pick up MC from underneath the CC **(B)**, p1 MC, hold MC in front and pick up CC from underneath the MC, p1 CC] 9 times. If you are turning the yarns in the right direction, you will notice that the yarns are untwisting themselves. Break the CC yarn and leave it hanging on the WS, k4 MC. The strands should run along the front of your knitting, i.e., the right side. You have completed the braid.

Continue with the MC.

**Row 9 (WS):** Sl1p, k3, p19, k4.
**Row 10 (RS):** Sl1p, k26.
**Rows 11–12:** Repeat Rows 9–10 once more.
**Row 13 (WS):** As Row 9.
**Rows 14–40:** Repeat Rows 6–13 another 3 times, then repeat Rows 6–8 once more (making one more braid).
**Row 41 (WS):** With MC sl1p, k3, p19, k4.

At this point you have 5 braids and 21 garter-st ridges on the right- and left-hand borders of the square.

**Rows 42–47:** Sl1p, k26.

Cast off and weave in ends.

 NOW YOU KNOW HOW TO

make a Latvian braid

# 26. The Magic One

## *How to slip the first stitch after a purl stitch*

Illusion knitting is a fun technique! This square, when viewed from the front, looks as if it has horizontal stripes, but when looked at from an angle it seems to have wide vertical stripes. The effect is achieved by using knit and purl stitches. You'll be amazed at the images you can create using this simple technique.

 YOU ALREADY KNOW HOW TO

- cast on, knit, and cast/bind off (**00**. The Basic One)
- slip the first stitch purlwise (**01**. The Slippy One)
- knit horizontal stripes (**02**. The Striped One)
- purl (**03**. The Purly One)
- follow a knitting pattern containing abbreviations (**04**. The Seedy One)

## Instructions

Using MC, cast on 27 sts.

**Row 1 (WS):** Sl1p, k5, p5, k5, p5, k6.
**Row 2 (RS):** With CC, sl1p, k to end of row.
**Row 3 (WS):** Sl1p, p5, k5, p5, k5, p6.
**Row 4 (RS):** With MC, sl1p, k to end of row.

Notice that this first st is slipped with the yarn in the back. No need for the purl manoeuver. Why? Check out the Geeky Notes for this technique.

**Row 5 (WS):** Sl1p, k5, p5, k5, p5, k6.
**Rows 6–45:** Repeat Rows 2–5 another 10 times.
**Rows 46–47:** Repeat Rows 2–3 once more.

You should now have 12 stripes in each colour.

Cast off and weave in ends.

### GEEKY NOTES 

**So what happened in Row 4, and why was this first stitch different from the ones you have slipped up to now?**

In the squares you have knitted so far, the last stitch of every row has always been a knit stitch. When slipping the first stitch, the yarn needs to be brought forward to continue knitting.

In Row 3, the last stitch is purled. In this case, you need to slip the first stitch with the yarn in the back, i.e., simply transfer the stitch from the LH to the RH needle without moving the yarn.

It is also possible, if the last stitch of your previous row was a purl stitch, to slip the stitch knitwise.

NOW YOU KNOW HOW TO
slip the first stitch after a purl stitch

See clips 27.1, 27.2.

# **27.** The Reversible One

## *How to work double knitting*

Double knitting creates two layers of fabric simultaneously with the same pattern, but with reversed colours. This is achieved by knitting the stitch of the front layer with one colour while holding the other yarn in the back and purling the stitch of the back layer with the second colour while holding the other yarn to the front.

### YOU ALREADY KNOW HOW TO

- cast on, knit, and cast/bind off (**00**. The Basic One)
- purl (**03**. The Purly One)
- follow a knitting pattern containing abbreviations (**04**. The Seedy One)
- read a knitting chart (**05**. The Charted One)
- make a left-leaning decrease (**08**. The Left One)
- make twisted-loop increases (**13**. The Loopy One)
- knit using the intarsia technique (**20**. The Square One)
- knit stranded colourwork on two needles (**22**. The Flat One)
- work the mosaic technique (**24**. The Mosaic One)

### CHART KEY

Each square represents 2 sts – a knit st and a purl st

☐ RS: k1 CC, p1 MC / WS: k1 MC, p1 CC

■ RS: k1 MC, p1 CC / WS: k1 CC, p1 MC

## Instructions

Using MC, cast on 27 sts.

**Rows 1–6:** Sl1p, k26.
**Row 7 (WS):** Sl1p, k3, p19, k4.
**Row 8 (RS):** Sl1p, k26.
**Rows 9–12:** Repeat Rows 7–8 twice more.
**Row 13 (WS):** As Row 7.

Row 14 is the set-up row for the double knitting section. You will cast on an extra series of sts for the second layer using backwards loops.

**Row 14 (RS):** Sl1p, k6, [k1, make backwards loop] 13 times, k7.

Rows 15–32 are worked in two colours. When knitting the double knitting section (shown in the chart) you should hold the knit st colour to the right. This means that you should switch the placement of the yarns between RS and WS rows. On Row 15 hold the MC to the right.

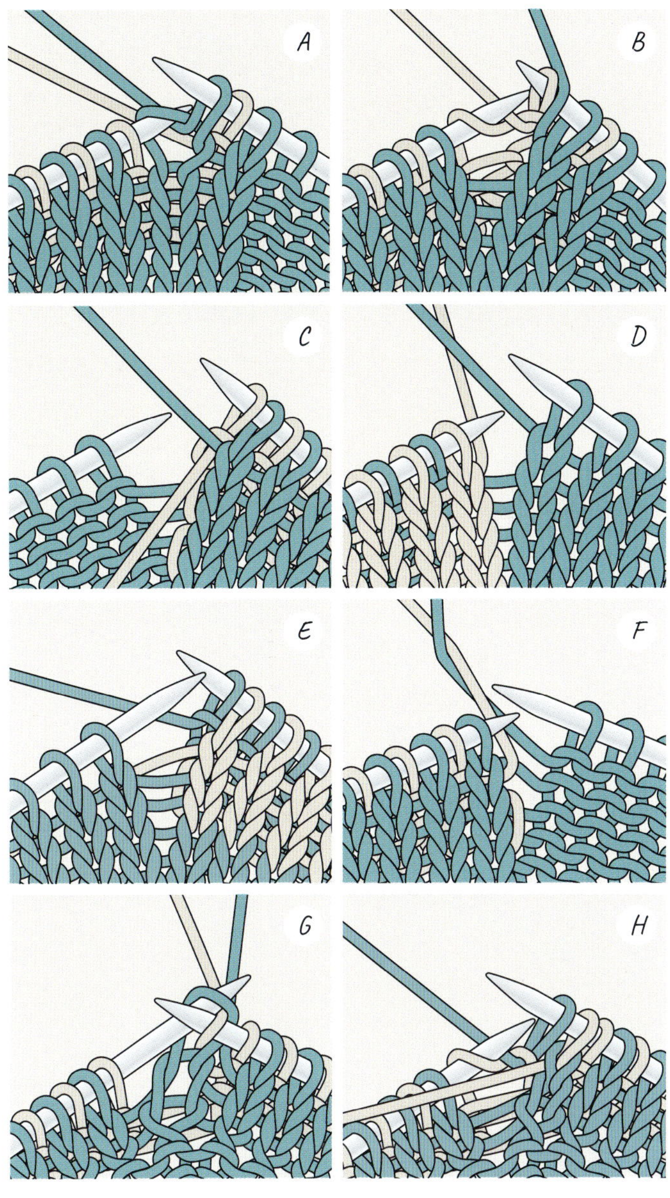


**Row 15 (WS):** Sl1p, k3, p3, work Row 1 of the chart over the next 13 double sts as follows: [k1 MC, p1 CC] 13 times **(A, B)**, bring CC to front under the MC yarn and leave it there **(C)**, with MC p3, k4.
**Row 16 (RS):** Sl1p, k6 MC, place yarns for double knitting with CC to the right and MC above it to the left **(D)** and work Row 2 of the chart over the next 13 double sts as follows: [k1 CC, p1 MC] 13 times, bring CC to back under the MC yarn and leave it there **(E)**, k7 MC.
**Row 17 (WS):** Sl1p, k3, p3, twist the yarns and place MC to the right **(F)**, work Row 3 of the chart over the next 13 double sts as follows: [k1 MC, p1 CC] 6 times, k1 CC **(G)**, p1 MC holding the CC yarn in front **(H)** so that it will lie between the 2 double-knitting layers, [k1 MC, p1 CC] 6 times, bring CC to front under the MC and leave it there, with MC, p3, k4.
**Row 18 (RS):** Sl1p, k6, place yarns for double knitting with CC to the right and MC above it to the left, work Row 4 of the chart over the next 13 double sts as follows: [k1 CC, p1 MC] 6 times, k1 MC, p1 CC holding the MC yarn in front, [k1 CC, p1 MC] 6 times, bring CC to back under MC yarn, k7 MC.
**Rows 19–32:** Continue in pattern as established, working Rows 5–18 of the chart.

Break CC yarn. Continue with MC.

**Row 33 (WS):** Sl1p, k3, p3, [k1, sl1p wyif] 13 times, p3, k4.
**Row 34 (RS):** Sl1p, k6, SSK 13 times, k7.
**Row 35 (WS):** Sl1p, k3, p19, k4.
**Row 36 (RS):** Sl1p, k26.
**Rows 37–40:** Repeat Rows 35–36 twice more.
**Row 41 (WS):** As Row 35.
**Rows 42–47:** As Row 36.

Cast off and weave in ends.

## If you are a thrower...

Move both yarns to the back and knit the next st with one colour, then move both yarns to the front and purl the next st with the other colour.

# 28. The Invisible One

## *How to catch floats with the invisible stranding technique*

Another way of catching floats is to cast on an extra stitch behind the work and purl this in every round with the colour not being used. This is completely invisible on the right side of the work, and creates a layer like a spider's web on the wrong side.

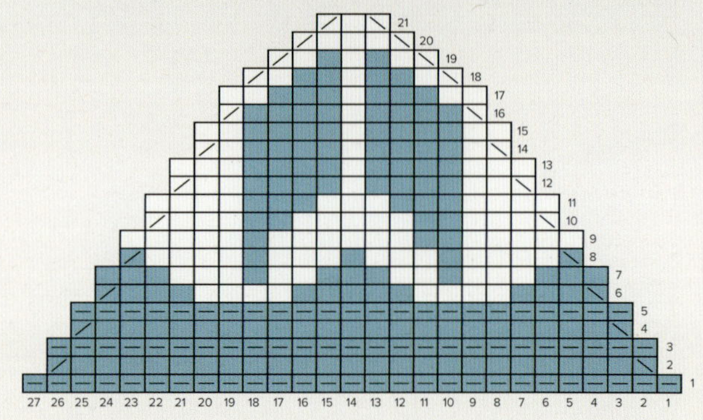


### CHART KEY

- MC
- CC
- k
- k2tog
- p
- SSK

### YOU ALREADY KNOW HOW TO

- cast on, knit, and cast/bind off (**00**. The Basic One)
- purl (**03**. The Purly One)
- abbreviations (**04**. The Seedy One)
- read a knitting chart (**05**. The Charted One)
- decrease by knitting two stitches together (**06**. The Mitred One)
- place and slip a marker (**06**. The Mitred One)
- make a left-leaning decrease (**08**. The Left One)
- knit or purl a stitch through the back loop (**09**. The Twisted One)
- work "make one" increases (**14**. The Neat One)
- make increases and decreases on purl rows (**15**. The Complicated One)
- knit in the round (**16**. The Circular One)
- knit jogless stripes in the round (**17**. The Jogless One)
- knit stranded colourwork in the round (**18**. The Stranded One)
- work double knitting (**27**. The Reversible One)

### EXTRA MATERIALS

- yarn in 2 different colours
- circular needles, 4mm (US size 6 or UK size 8), 40cm/16in long
- 5 DPNs, 4mm (US size 6 or UK size 8)
- 4 stitch markers, one of which should be different to the rest to mark the beginning of the round

*Back of square*

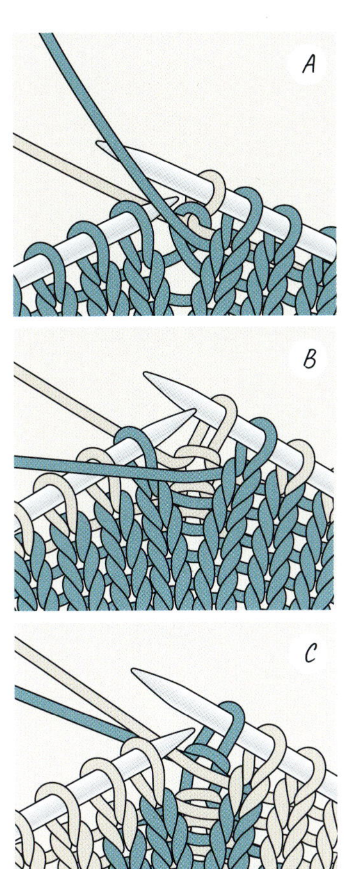


## Instructions

Using circular needles and MC yarn, cast on 108 sts. Join in the round and PM to mark the beginning of the round. Take care not to twist your sts.

**Rnd 1:** Purl, PM after every 27th st.
**Rnd 2:** [SSK, k to 2 sts before marker, k2tog, SM] 4 times. (8 sts decreased)
**Rnd 3:** Purl.
**Rnd 4:** As Rnd 2. (92 sts)
**Rnd 5:** Purl.

Begin colourwork on Rnd 6, holding MC dominant throughout. On this round you will make 4 extra sts, which will lie behind the work. These extra sts are not shown in the chart. They are purled behind the work much as in double knitting.

**Rnd 6:** [Work Row 6 of the chart once, SM, holding MC in front M1pL with CC **(A)**] 4 times. (88 sts)
**Rnd 7:** [Work Row 7 of the chart once, SM, holding MC in front p1 with CC **(B)**] 4 times.
**Rnd 8:** [Work Row 8 of the chart once, SM, holding MC in front p1 with CC] 4 times. (80 sts)

From Rnd 9 onwards, you will need to catch the MC yarn instead.

**Rnd 9:** [Work Row 9 of the chart once, SM, holding CC in front p1 with MC **(C)**] 4 times.
**Rnds 10–12:** Continue according to chart, decreasing as shown and working p1 with MC as on Rnd 9. (64 sts)

Transfer sts to DPNs and remove markers on Rnd 13 as follows:

**Rnd 13:** [Work Row 13 of the chart onto a DPN, RM, change DPN, holding CC in front p1 with MC] 3 times, work Row 13 of the chart onto the fourth DPN, RM, transfer the last extra st of the rnd onto the first DPN (now each extra st is at the beginning of a DPN).
**Rnd 14:** [Holding CC in front, p1 with MC, work Row 14 of the chart] 4 times. (56 sts)
**Rnd 15:** [With CC, k2tog (first st with first chart st), work remaining sts from Row 15 of the chart] 4 times. (52 sts)
**Rnds 16–21:** Continue according to chart. (12 sts)

Break both yarns. Pass the CC yarn through the remaining sts. Pull the yarn to close the hole tightly and weave in the ends.

**NOW YOU KNOW HOW TO**
catch floats with the invisible stranding technique

# **29.** The Parallel One

## *How to work the roosimine technique*

Roosimine is an Estonian technique that creates patterns by making floats in another colour on the right side of your knitting. You may also see it referred to as “roositud”. “Roosimine” describes the action, while “roositud” refers to the result of the technique.

### YOU ALREADY KNOW HOW TO

- cast on, knit, and cast/bind off (**00**. The Basic One)
- slip the first stitch purlwise (**01**. The Slippy One)
- purl (**03**. The Purly One)
- follow a knitting pattern containing abbreviations (**04**. The Seedy One)
- read a knitting chart (**05**. The Charted One)
- decrease by knitting two stitches together (**06**. The Mitred One)
- make a left-leaning decrease (**08**. The Left One)
- knit in the round (**16**. The Circular One)

### EXTRA MATERIALS

- 4 x 150cm/60in of CC yarn
- circular needles, 4mm (US size 6 or UK size 8), 40cm/16in long
- 5 DPNs, 4mm (US size6 or UK size 8)
- 4 stitch markers, one of which should be different to the rest to mark the beginning of the round

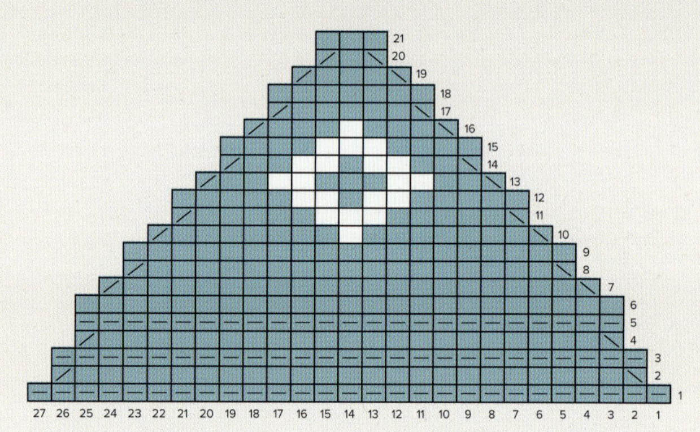


### CHART KEY

- MC
- CC
- k
- k2tog
- p
- SSK

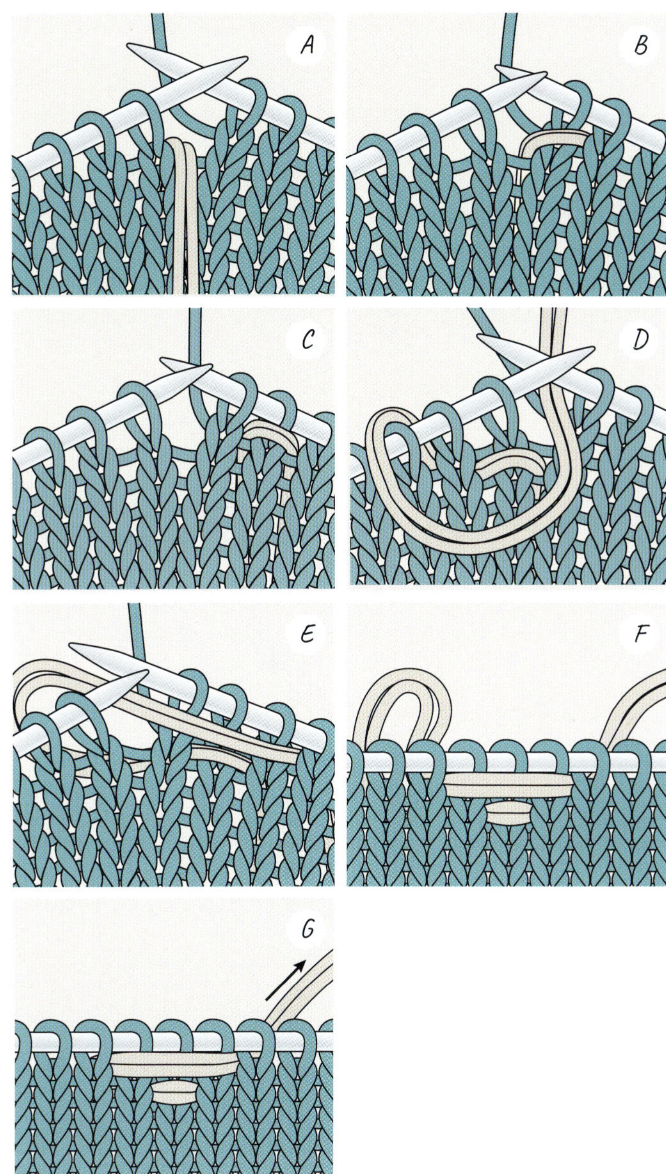


## Instructions

Using circular needles and MC, cast on 108 sts. Join in the round and PM to mark the beginning of the round. Take care not to twist your sts.

**Rnd 1:** Purl, PM after every 27th st.
**Rnd 2:** [SSK, k to 2 sts before marker, k2tog, SM] 4 times. (8 sts decreased)
**Rnd 3:** Purl.
**Rnd 4:** As Rnd 2. (92 sts)
**Rnd 5:** Purl.
**Rnd 6:** Knit.
**Rnd 7:** As Rnd 2. (84 sts)
**Rnd 8:** As Rnd 2. (76 sts)
**Rnd 9:** Knit.

The roosimine technique starts on Rnd 10. Each diamond is made with a separate double strand of CC yarn.

Take a length of CC yarn approx 150cm/60in. Fold it in half.

**Rnd 10:** [SSK, k7, take one of the folded strands and lay it between your needles with the short tail at the back of the work **(A)**, k1 with MC, take the CC yarn and lay it behind the work under the working yarn **(B)**, k7 with MC **(C)**, k2tog] 4 times. (68 sts)
**Rnd 11:** [SSK, k5, bring the long end of the CC yarn of this diamond over the LH needle to the front, leave a long loop hanging in the front of the work and place the yarn between the needles with the end to the back **(D)**, k3, now take the loop with your left hand and place the yarn between your needles **(E)**, k5, SSK, k2tog. Pull the CC yarn end with your right hand until floats lie snugly but not too tightly on the RS **(F, G)**] 4 times. (60 sts)
**Rnd 12:** [K5, bring CC yarn to the front, k2, take CC yarn to the back, k1, bring CC yarn to the front, k2, take CC yarn to the back, k5] 4 times.
**Rnds 13–21:** Continue according to chart, working each chart row 4 times on every round and decreasing as indicated. On odd-numbered rows, the CC yarn will be on the left side of the motif, so you need to make a large loop, as described on Rnd 11. On even-numbered rows, simply carry the yarn from right to left as you knit. Transfer the sts to DPNs on Rnd 13.

After completing Rnd 21, you should have 12 sts. Break the yarn and pass it through the remaining sts. Pull the yarn to close the hole tightly and weave in the ends.

See clip 30.1.

# **30.** The Backwards One

## *How to knit backwards and how to make bobbles*

Bobbles are a fun way to embellish your knits. A typical bobble is made by knitting back and forth over a few stitches. You will notice there's a lot of turning your project, but you can avoid that by learning to knit backwards.

### YOU ALREADY KNOW HOW TO

- cast on, knit, and cast/bind off (**00**. The Basic One)
- slip the first stitch purlwise (**01**. The Slippy One)
- purl (**03**. The Purly One)
- follow a knitting pattern containing abbreviations (**04**. The Seedy One)
- read a knitting chart (**05**. The Charted One)
- make a double decrease (**11**. The Convergent One)
- make a double increase (**12**. The Budding One)

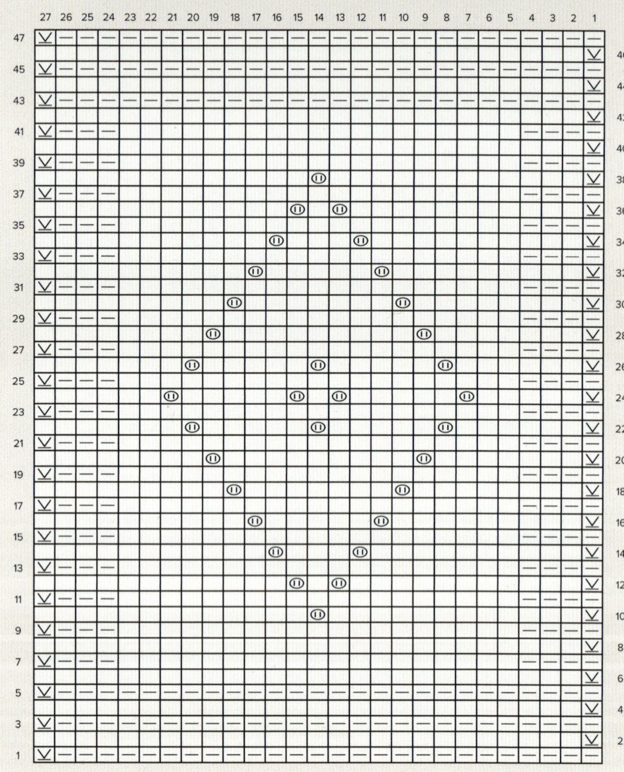

CHART KEY

- Bobble
- RS: k / WS: p
- RS: p / WS: k
- Sl1p

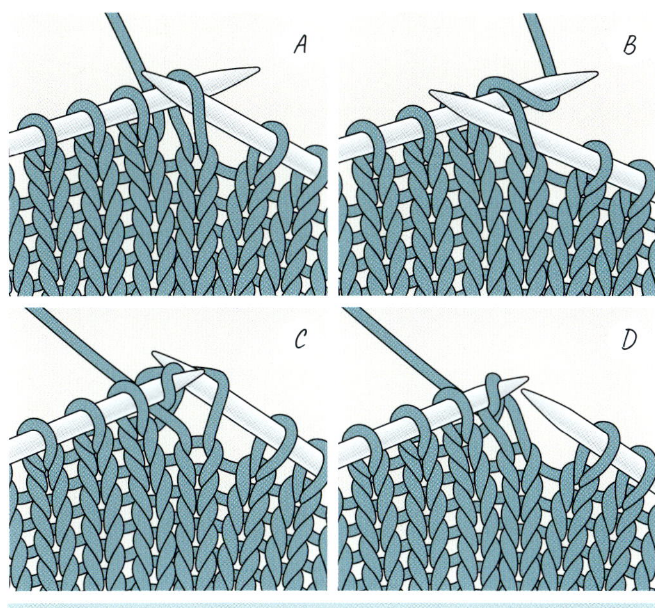


## Instructions

Cast on 27 sts.

**Rows 1–6:** Sl1p, k26.
**Row 7 (WS):** Sl1p, k3, p19, k4.
**Row 8 (RS):** As Row 6.
**Row 9 (WS):** As Row 7.
**Row 10 (RS):** Sl1p, k12, make bobble as follows: kyok, turn your work to have the WS facing you, p3, turn your work back again to have the RS facing you, CDD. Knit to end of row.
**Row 11 (WS):** As Row 7.

On Row 12 you will make your next bobble. This time I suggest you try knitting backwards as follows: kyok, k3 backwards, k3 forwards, CDD.

**Row 12 (RS):** Sl1p, k11, make bobble, k1, make bobble, k12.

**To knit a st backwards:** insert the LH needle tip into the st on your RH needle **(A)**, wrap the working yarn around the LH needle tip with your left hand **(B)**, then use the RH needle tip to pull the st over the yarn **(C)**. The completed st is on your LH needle **(D)**.

**Rows 13–47:** Continue according to chart.

Cast off and weave in ends.

### If you are a thrower...

When knitting backwards, I knit English style mirrored. I do this so as not to change the position of the yarn. So, if you are a thrower, you can either knit backwards this way, or you can leave the working yarn on your right hand and mirror the Continental style.

### *Anna's tips...*

Tighten the yarn as soon as you have completed the bobble to avoid creating a big gap. Also tighten the yarn in the next row when you knit over the bobble.

See clip 31.1.

# 31. The Knobbly One

## *How to close the gap next to a bobble*

The previous bobbles were made using the kyok multiple increase. The kfbfb is also used quite frequently in bobbles. This increase, however, leaves an enormous hole next to the bobble. It is possible to close this gap in the next row or round.

### YOU ALREADY KNOW HOW TO

- cast on, knit, and cast/bind off (**00**. The Basic One)
- purl (**03**. The Purly One)
- follow a knitting pattern containing abbreviations (**04**. The Seedy One)
- decrease by knitting two stitches together (**06**. The Mitred One)
- place and slip a marker (**06**. The Mitred One)
- make a left-leaning decrease (**08**. The Left One)
- slip a stitch knitwise (**08**. The Left One)
- make a kfb increase (**10**. The Diagonal One)
- make a double decrease (**11**. The Convergent One)
- make a double increase (**12**. The Budding One)
- work "make one" increases (**14**. The Neat One)
- knit in the round (**16**. The Circular One)
- slip the first stitch after a purl stitch (**26**. The Magic One)
- knit backwards (**30**. The Backwards One)
- make bobbles (**30**. The Backwards One)

### NEW ABBREVIATIONS

**kfbfb:** knit front, back, front, back
**p2sso:** pass two slipped stitches over
**sl2tog:** slip two stitches together

### EXTRA MATERIALS

- circular needles, 4mm (US size 6 or UK size 8), 40cm/16in long
- 5 DPNs, 4mm (US size 6 or UK size 8)
- 4 stitch markers, one of which should be different to the rest to mark the beginning of the round

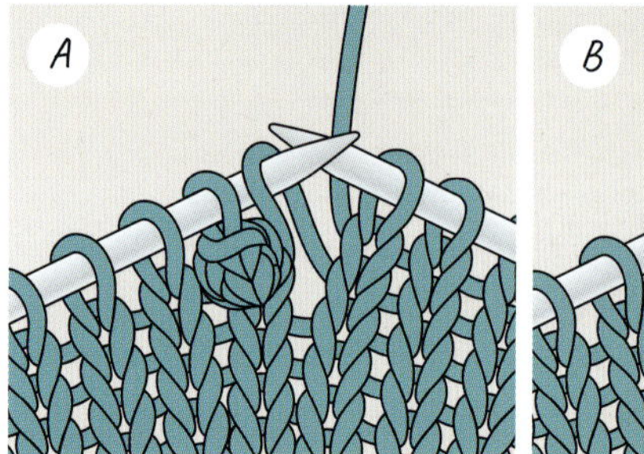


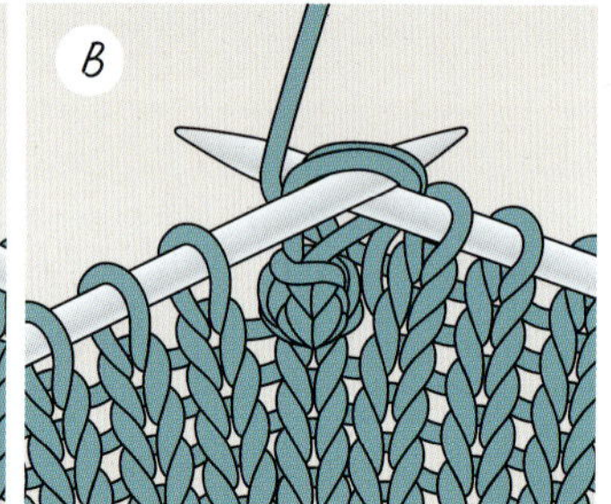


### GEEKY NOTES

This trick can be used to close any unwanted gaps that appear in your projects. Such gaps typically appear at the armholes on top-down sweaters or at the corners of the heel in socks.

## Instructions

Using circular needles, cast on 108 sts. Join in the round and PM to mark the beginning of the round. Take care not to twist your sts.

**Rnd 1:** Purl, PM after every 27th st.
**Rnd 2:** [SSK, k to 2 sts before marker, k2tog, SM] 4 times. (8 sts decreased)
**Rnd 3:** Purl.
**Rnd 4:** As Rnd 2. (92 sts)
**Rnd 5:** Purl.
**Rnd 6:** Knit.
**Rnd 7:** As Rnd 2. (84 sts)
**Rnd 8:** As Rnd 2. (76 sts)
**Rnd 9:** Knit.
**Rnd 10:** As Rnd 2. (68 sts)
**Rnd 11:** As Rnd 2. (60 sts)
**Rnd 12:** Knit, transferring the sts to DPNs and removing markers.
**Rnd 13:** As Rnd 2. (52 sts)
**Rnd 14:** As Rnd 2. (44 sts)
**Rnd 15:** Knit.
**Rnd 16:** [SSK, k7, k2tog] 4 times. (36 sts)
**Rnd 17:** [SSK, k5, k2tog] 4 times. (28 sts)
**Rnd 18:** Knit.
**Rnd 19:** [SSK, k3, k2tog] 4 times. (20 sts)
**Rnd 20:** [SSK, make bobble, k2tog] 4 times. (12 sts)

**Make bobble as follows:** Kfbfb, turn, sl1p, p3, turn, sl1p, k3, turn, sl1p, p3, turn, sl2tog knitwise, SSK, p2sso.

**Rnd 21:** In this rnd, close the gaps before the bobbles as follows: [k1, lift up the bar between the sts onto the LH needle with the left leg in front **(A)**, knit it together with the next st (the st of the bobble) **(B)**, k1] 4 times.

Break the yarn and pass it through the remaining sts. Pull the yarn to close the hole tightly and weave in the ends.

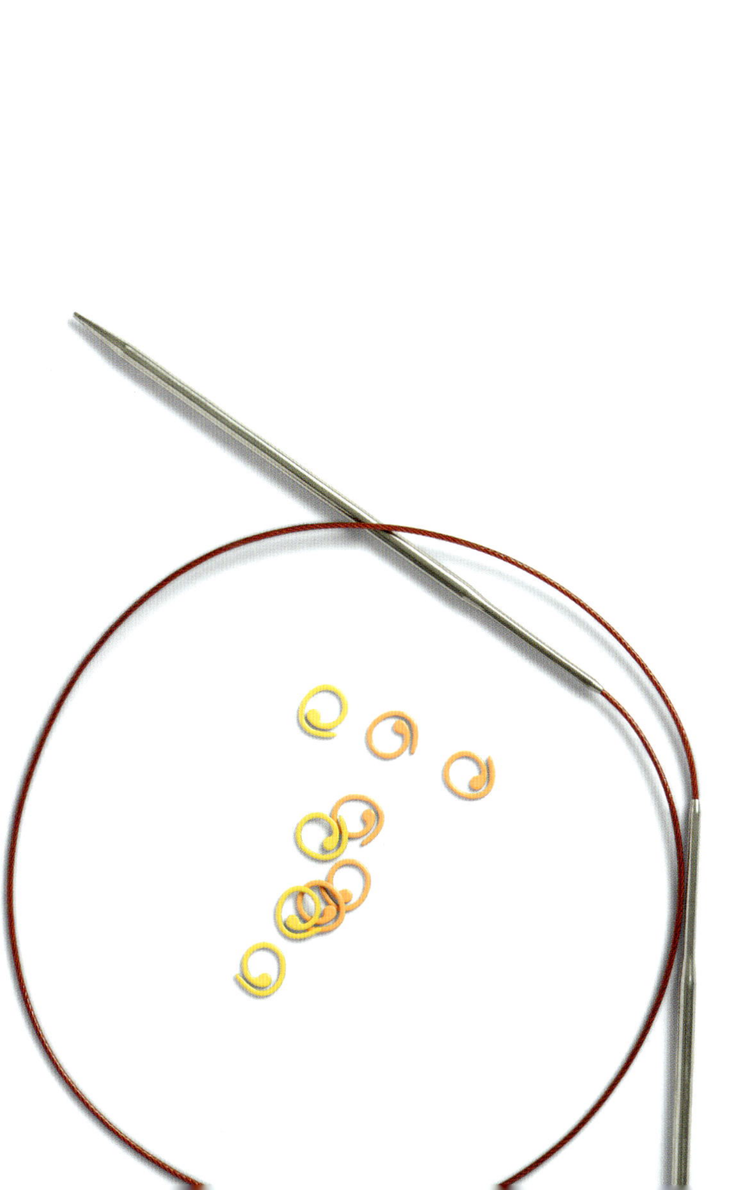

**NOW YOU KNOW HOW TO**
close the gap next to a bobble

See clip 32.1.

# 32. The Knotty One

## *How to close gaps on wrong-side rows*

The previous square was knitted in the round. If you are knitting flat, the holes around the bobbles need to be closed on the following row, which is a wrong-side row.

### YOU ALREADY KNOW HOW TO

- cast on, knit, and cast/bind off (**00**. The Basic One)
- slip the first stitch purlwise (**01**. The Slippy One)
- purl (**03**. The Purly One)
- follow a knitting pattern containing abbreviations (**04**. The Seedy One)
- read a knitting chart (**05**. The Charted One)
- decrease by knitting two stitches together (**06**. The Mitred One)
- make a kfb increase (**10**. The Diagonal One)
- make increases and decreases on purl rows (**15**. The Complicated One)
- knit backwards (**30**. The Backwards One)
- make bobbles (**30**. The Backwards One)
- close the gap next to a bobble (**31**. The Knobbly One)

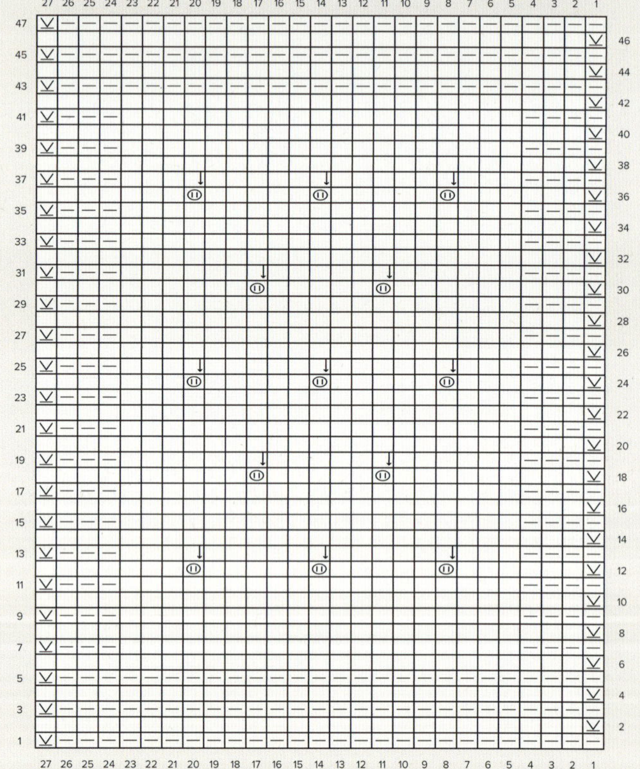

### CHART KEY

- Bobble
- RS: k / WS: p
- RS: p / WS: k
- Sl1p

Arrow shows where to pick up the strand between sts and purl tog with the previous st to close the gap next to the bobble.

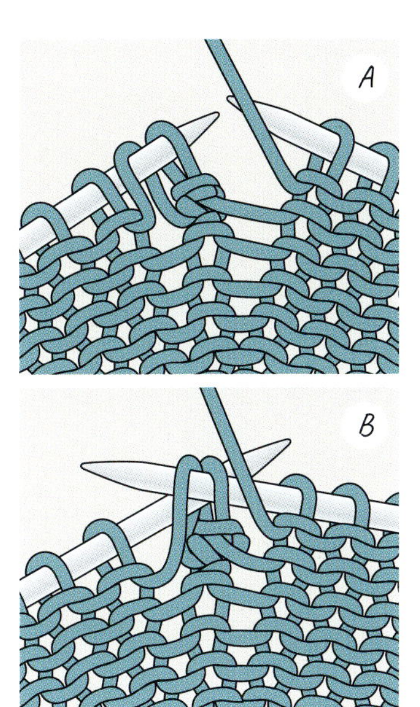


## Instructions

Cast on 27 sts.

**Rows 1–6:** Sl1p, k26.
**Row 7 (WS):** Sl1p, k3, p19, k4.
**Row 8 (RS):** Sl1p, k26.
**Rows 9–10:** Repeat Rows 7 and 8 once more.
**Row 11 (WS):** As Row 7.

On Row 12 you will make a knot and on Row 13 you will close the gap it created.

**Row 12 (RS):** Sl1p, k6, make knot, [K5, make knot] twice, k7.

**To make a knot:** kfb, turn, p2, turn, k2tog.

**To close the gap on the next row:** sl next st (the knot st) to the RH needle, lift up the horizontal bar between the needles onto the LH needle with the left leg in front, sl the knot st back onto the LH needle **(A)** and purl it together with the loop on your LH needle **(B)**.

**Row 13 (WS):** Sl1p, k3, p3, [close the gap, p5] twice, close the gap, p3, k4.

**Rows 14–47:** Continue according to chart.

Cast off and weave in ends.

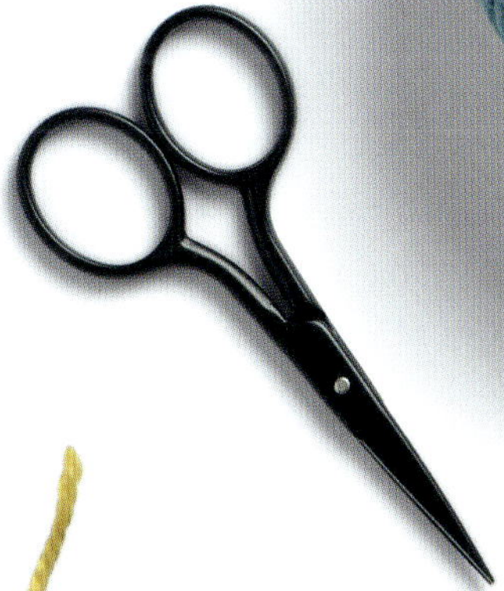

*NOW YOU KNOW HOW TO*

close gaps on wrong-side rows

See clips 33.1, 33.2.

# 33. The Ropey One

## *How to knit rope cables*

Cables are another fun embellishing technique. They are made by crossing stitches, usually with the help of an extra needle.

### YOU ALREADY KNOW HOW TO

- cast on, knit, and cast/bind off (**00**. The Basic One)
- slip the first stitch purlwise (**01**. The Slippy One)
- purl (**03**. The Purly One)
- follow a knitting pattern containing abbreviations (**04**. The Seedy One)
- read a knitting chart (**05**. The Charted One)
- decrease by knitting two stitches together (**06**. The Mitred One)
- knit or purl a stitch through the back loop (**09**. The Twisted One)
- work "make one" increases (**14**. The Neat One)

### EXTRA MATERIALS

- a cable needle or DPN

### NEW ABBREVIATIONS

**cn:** cable needle
**C6B:** cable 6 back, i.e., 6-st right-twisting cable
**C6F:** cable 6 front, i.e., 6-st left-twisting cable

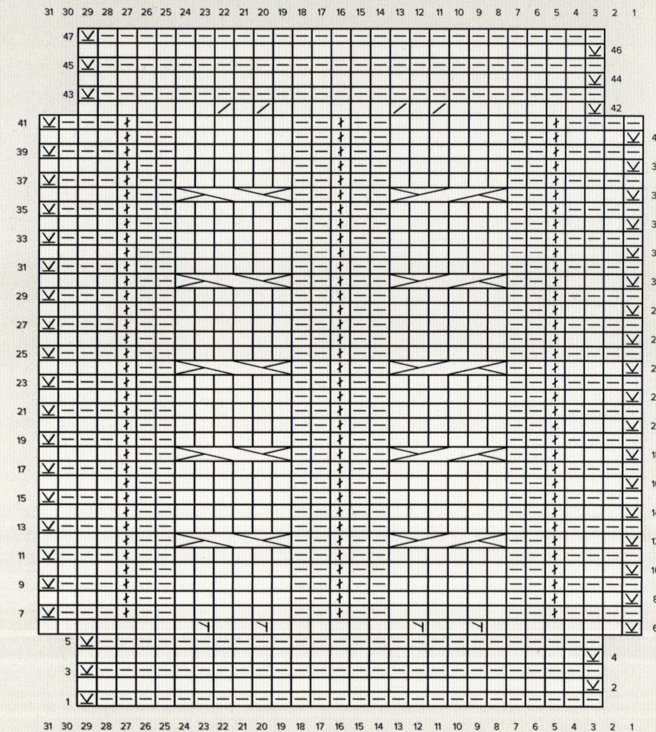

### CHART KEY

C6B
C6F
RS: k / WS: p
RS: k1 tbl / WS: p1 tbl
k2tog
M1L
RS: p / WS: k
Sl1p

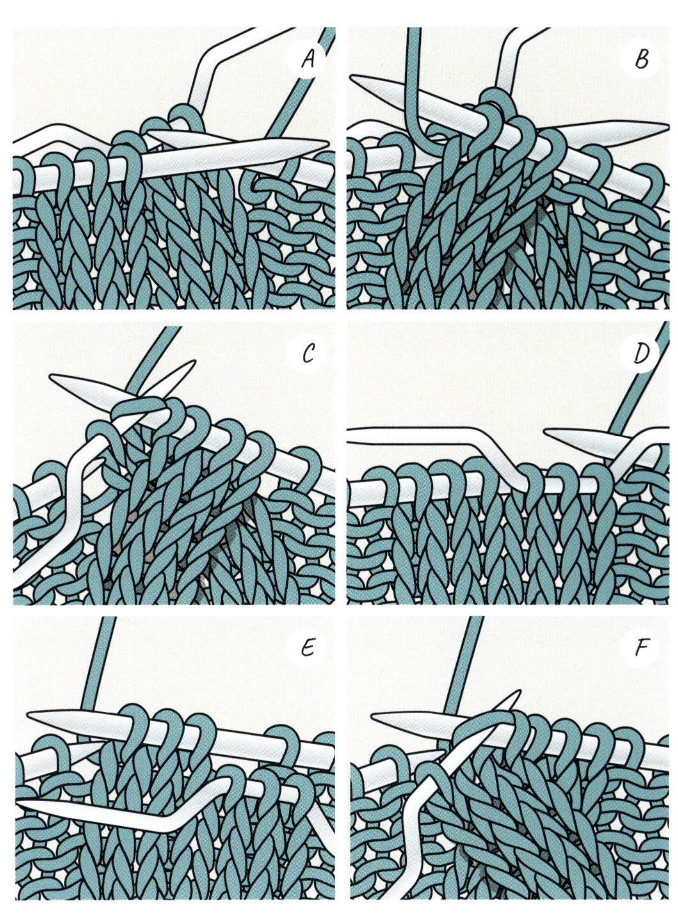


## Instructions

Cast on 27 sts.

**Rows 1–5:** Sl1p, k26.
**Row 6 (RS):** Sl1p, k7, M1L, k2, M1L, k7, M1L, k2, M1L, k8. (31 sts)
**Row 7 (WS):** Sl1p, k3, p1 tbl, k2, p6, k2, p1 tbl, k2, p6, k2, p1 tbl, k4.
**Row 8 (RS):** Sl1p, k3, k1 tbl, p2, k6, p2, k1 tbl, p2, k6, p2, k 1tbl, k4.
**Rows 9–10:** Repeat Rows 7–8 once more.
**Row 11 (WS):** As Row 7.
**Row 12 (RS):** Sl1p, k3, k1 tbl, p2, C6B, p2, k1 tbl, p2, C6F, p2, k1 tbl, k4.

**To make a C6B:** sl next 3 sts onto a cn **(A)**, leave at back of work, k next 3 sts **(B)**, k3 from cn **(C)**.

**To make a C6F:** sl next 3 sts onto a cn, leave at front of work **(D)**, k next 3 sts **(E)**, k3 from cn **(F)**.

**Rows 13–47:** Continue according to chart.

Cast off and weave in ends.

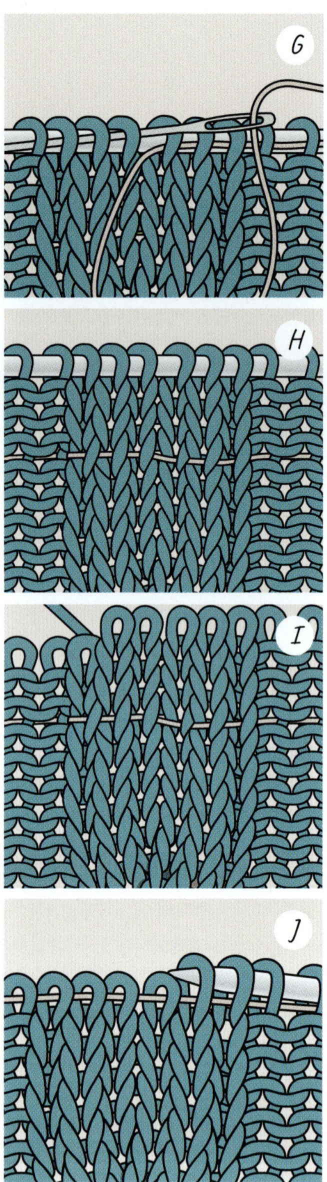


## Anna's tips... 

- When knitting complex patterns, such as cables or lace, you can add a lifeline. These patterns are difficult to unravel neatly, and, without a lifeline to "catch" you, you may end up frogging the whole of your work. Even experienced knitters have finished a whole garment, only to find that they have crossed a cable the wrong way.
  - To add a lifeline: a couple of rows before you need to cross your cables, pass a piece of thin, slippery yarn (I like to use unwaxed dental floss) through all the stitches **(G)**. Make sure that the yarn is lying at the base of the stitches and that you have not sewn through the knitting yarn. Knit normally, ignoring the lifeline **(H)**. If something goes wrong, you can easily frog your knitting down to the lifeline **(I)**, mount the stitches onto a knitting needle **(J)** and continue knitting from there. When you are done knitting, simply pull the lifeline out.
- Things tend to get a bit fiddly with cable needles. There are alternatives you might like to try, e.g., you can use a bobby pin, a safety pin or a stitch marker. You cannot, however, knit the stitches directly off any of these, so you have to slip the stitches back onto the left-hand needle to knit them. I normally cross the cables without a cable needle, especially when crossing only two stitches, as in the next square. To do this, pinch the base of the stitches, when you take them off the needle, so they do not unravel. If you are not very experienced, you may prefer not to try this technique.
- This square tends to pull together widthways. Make sure to place it somewhere in the middle of the throw, so the surrounding squares can pull it into shape (see Placement).

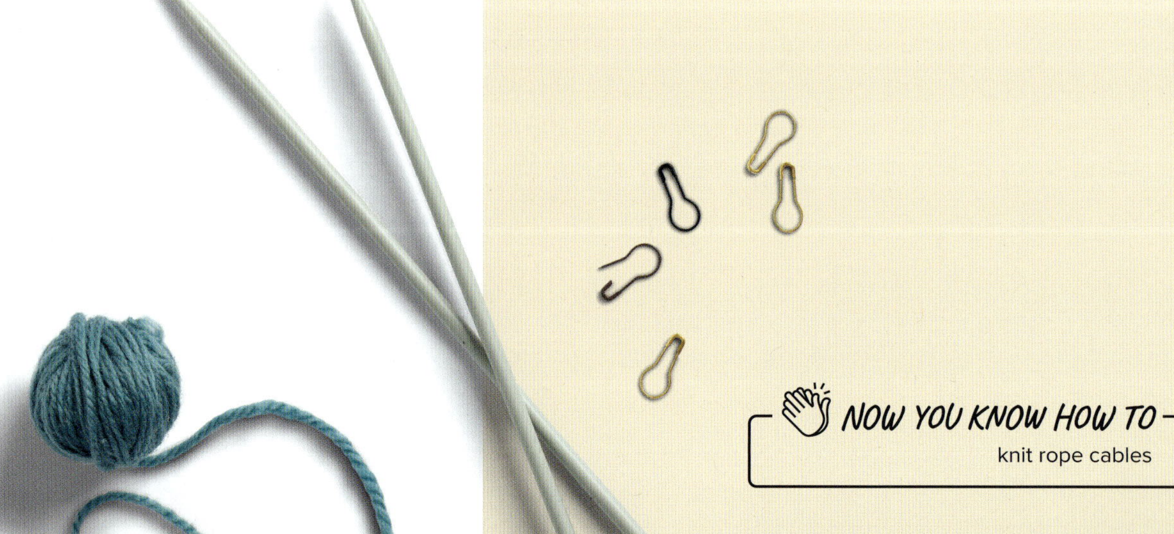

**NOW YOU KNOW HOW TO**

knit rope cables

# 34. The Latticed One

### *How to cross purl and twisted stitches*

In the previous square, you crossed knit stitches, but it's possible to cross any combination of stitches. In this square, you'll be crossing purl stitches and stitches knitted through the back loop.

## YOU ALREADY KNOW HOW TO

- cast on, knit, and cast/bind off (**00**. The Basic One)
- slip the first stitch purlwise (**01**. The Slippy One)
- purl (**03**. The Purly One)
- follow a knitting pattern containing abbreviations (**04**. The Seedy One)
- read a knitting chart (**05**. The Charted One)
- decrease by knitting two stitches together (**06**. The Mitred One)
- make a left-leaning decrease (**08**. The Left One)
- knit or purl a stitch through the back loop (**09**. The Twisted One)
- work "make one" increases (**14**. The Neat One)
- knit rope cables (**33**. The Ropey One)

## EXTRA MATERIALS

- a cable needle or removable stitch marker

## Instructions

Cast on 27 sts.

**Rows 1–5:** Sl1p, k26.
**Row 6 (RS):** Sl1p, k8, M1L, k2, M1L, k5, M1L, k2, M1L, k9. (31 sts)
**Row 7 (WS):** Sl1p, k5, [p1 tbl, k2] 7 times, k4.
**Row 8 (RS):** Sl1p, k3, [p2, k1 tbl, p2, sl next st to cn and hold at front, p1, k st from cn tbl, sl next st to cn and hold at back, k next st tbl, p1 from cn] twice, p2, k1 tbl, p2, k4.
**Row 9 (WS):** Sl1p, k5, [p1 tbl, k3, p2 tbl, k3] twice, p1 tbl, k6.
**Rows 10–47:** Continue according to chart.

Cast off and weave in ends.

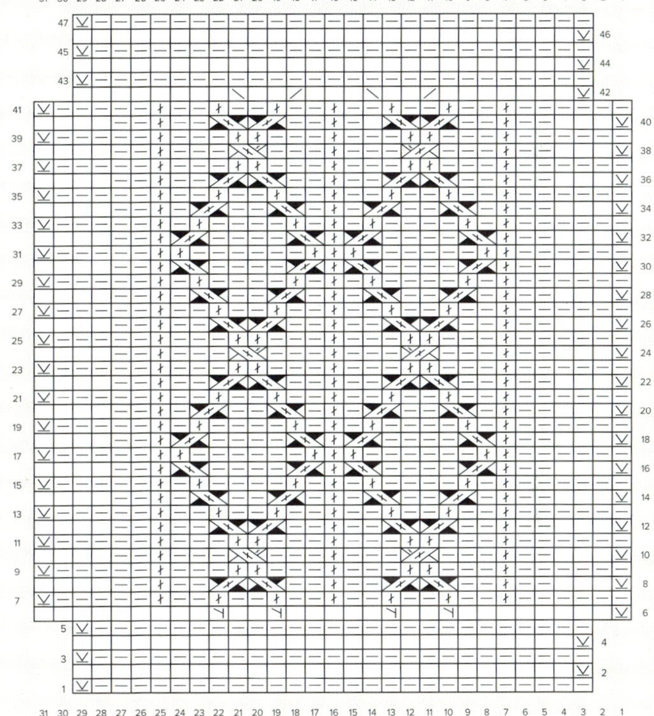

## CHART KEY

- RS: k2tog / WS: p2tog
- RS: k / WS: p
- RS: p / WS: k
- RS: k1 tbl / WS: p1 tbl
- RS: M1L / WS: M1pL
- Sl1 to cn, hold at front, p1, k1 tbl from cn
- Sl1 to cn, hold at back, k1 tbl, p1 from cn
- Sl1 to cn, hold at back, k1 tbl, k1 tbl from cn
- Sl1 to cn, hold at front, k1 tbl, k1 tbl from cn
- Sl1p
- RS: SSK / WS: SSP

## NOW YOU KNOW HOW TO

cross purl and twisted stitches

See clips 35.1, 35.2

# 35. The Faux One

## *How to make mock cable twists*

It's possible to make single stitch twists without technically crossing the stitches. This is an easy way to achieve the same effect, without having stitches hanging in mid-air.

### YOU ALREADY KNOW HOW TO

- cast on, knit, and cast/bind off (**00**. The Basic One)
- slip the first stitch purlwise (**01**. The Slippy One)
- purl (**03**. The Purly One)
- follow a knitting pattern containing abbreviations (**04**. The Seedy One)
- read a knitting chart (**05**. The Charted One)
- decrease by knitting two stitches together (**06**. The Mitred One)
- make a left-leaning decrease (**08**. The Left One)
- slip a stitch knitwise (**08**. The Left One)
- knit or purl a stitch through the back loop (**09**. The Twisted One)
- make a kfb increase (**10**. The Diagonal One)

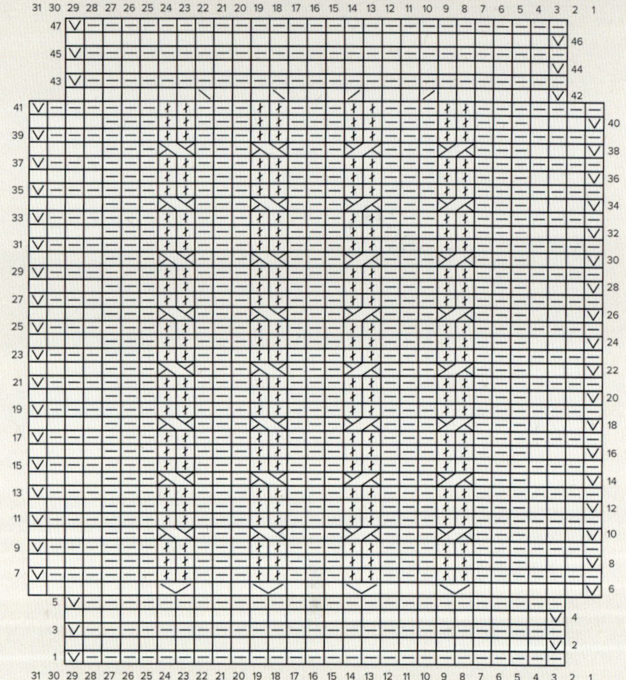

CHART KEY

- RS: k / WS: p
- k2tog
- kfb
- RS: k1 tbl / WS: p1 tbl
- Left twist
- Right twist
- RS: p / WS: k
- Sl1p
- SSK

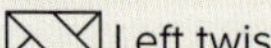

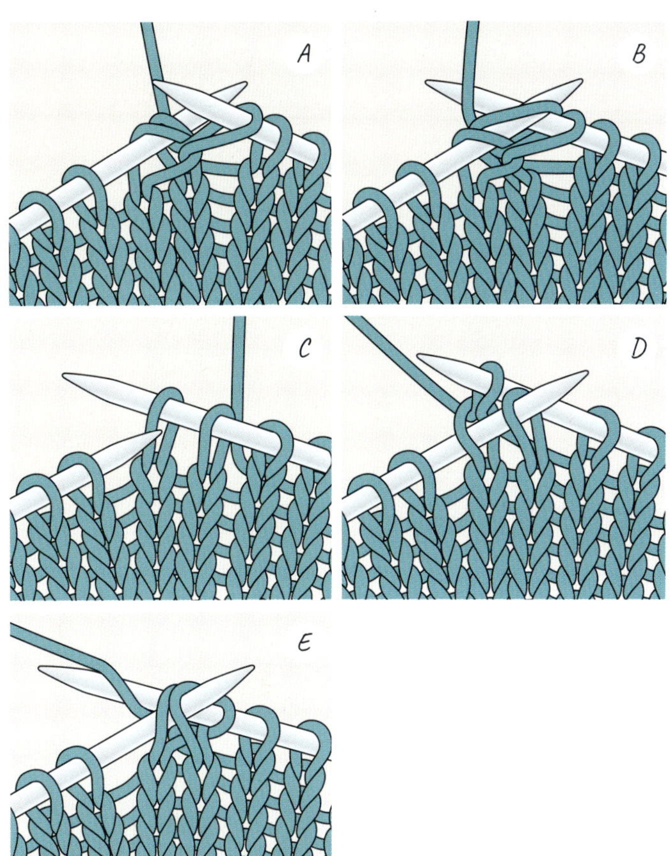


## Instructions

Cast on 27 sts.

**Rows 1–5:** Sl1p, k26.
**Row 6 (RS):** Sl1p, k6, [kfb, k3] 4 times, k4. (31 sts)
**Row 7 (WS):** Sl1p, k6, [p2 tbl, k3] 4 times, k4.
**Row 8 (RS):** Sl1p, k3, p3, [k2 tbl, p3] 4 times, k4.
**Row 9 (WS):** As Row 7.
**Row 10 (RS):** Sl1p, k3, [p3, make right twist] twice, p3 [make left twist, p3] twice, k4.

**To make a right twist:** knit 2 sts together without slipping them off the LH needle **(A)**, then knit the first st only and sl both sts off the LH needle **(B)**.

**To make a left twist:** sl next 2 sts knitwise **(C)** and place them back on the LH needle (as with SSK), knit into the back of the second st leaving it on the LH needle **(D)**, then knit both sts together **(E)** and sl them off the LH needle.

**Rows 11–47:** Continue according to chart.

Cast off and weave in ends.

### GEEKY NOTES 

This method produces a less stretchy fabric than when you actually cross the stitches, so, depending on the result you want to achieve, you may choose one method over the other.

See clip 36.1.

# 36. The Embroidered One

## *How to work the duplicate stitch*

Embroidery is another option for embellishing your knits. You can use any type of stitch. One type of stitch, however, is peculiar to knitting: the duplicate stitch, which mimics the knit stitch.

### YOU ALREADY KNOW HOW TO

- cast on, knit, and cast/bind off (**00**. The Basic One)
- slip the first stitch purlwise (**01**. The Slippy One)
- purl (**03**. The Purly One)

### EXTRA MATERIALS

- approx 1.8m/70in of CC yarn

### CHART KEY

- RS: k / WS: p
- RS: p / WS: k
- MC
- CC (work using embroidery on finished square)

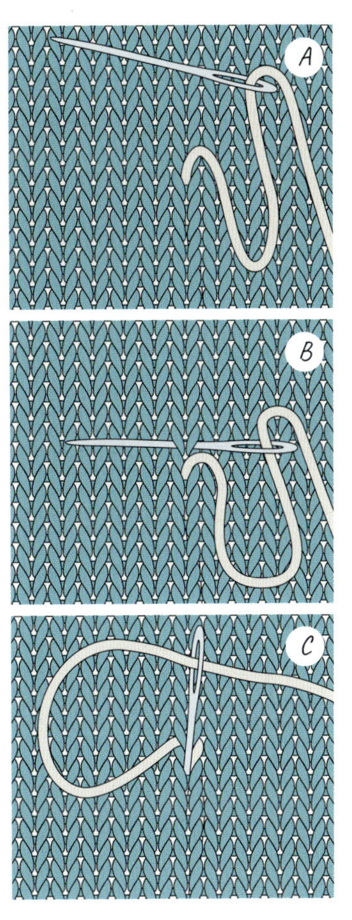


# Instructions

Knit a square in stocking st with a garter-st border as in **03.** The Purly One.

Embroider the motif according to the chart. The yarn should follow the shape of the knitted sts, i.e., each st forms a V. This is more or less the method you use when weaving in ends in stocking st. However, in this case you work on the right side and want the yarn to be visible and to cover the st below it as much as possible.

**To embroider a st:** bring up the tapestry needle from the back at the base of the st you want to cover **(A)**. Then follow the path of the st **(B)** and bring the needle down again through the same hole **(C)**. Bring the needle up again at the base of the next st you want to cover.

In the chart I have marked the order in which I suggest you embroider the sts.

When you finish the embroidery, weave in the ends – no knots allowed in knitting or embroidery!

## GEEKY NOTES

For some patterns, neither intarsia nor stranded knitting are suitable techniques. Embroidery is another option. However, the embroidered fabric gets rather thick. This may or may not be desirable, depending on what you are making.

work the duplicate stitch

# 37. The Logged One

## *How to pick up stitches*

Instead of knitting up stitches, you can also pick up loops out of the knitted fabric and then knit them. This square mimics a traditional quilting pattern called the log cabin. It consists of different sections. The central square is knitted first. Every time a section is completed, you pick up stitches along its left side to knit the next section.

### YOU ALREADY KNOW HOW TO

- cast on, knit, and cast/bind off (**00**. The Basic One)
- slip the first stitch purlwise (**01**. The Slippy One)
- follow a knitting pattern containing abbreviations (**04**. The Seedy One)

### EXTRA MATERIALS

- yarn in at least 2 different colours
- 2 DPNs

## Instructions

The sections are knitted in numerical order **(A)**.

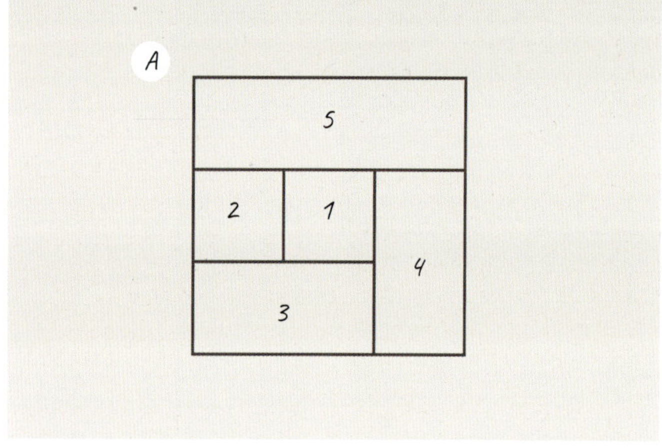


### Section 1 (central square)

Using CC cast on 9 sts.

**Rows 1–17:** Sl1p, k8.

You should now have 9 garter ridges on the RS. Cast off.

### Section 2 (left square)

Notice that the slipped selvedge sts form a chain along the sides of the square. Using a DPN and the MC, pick up 9 sts along the left edge.

**To pick up sts:** pick up the back leg of each sl st, i.e., the leg on the WS **(B)**. Notice that when you do this, the sts on the needle will have the "wrong" leg in front (the left leg). Knit these sts through the back loop (the right leg) so as not to twist them. If you have difficulty pulling the yarn through with the knitting needle, you can use a crochet hook.

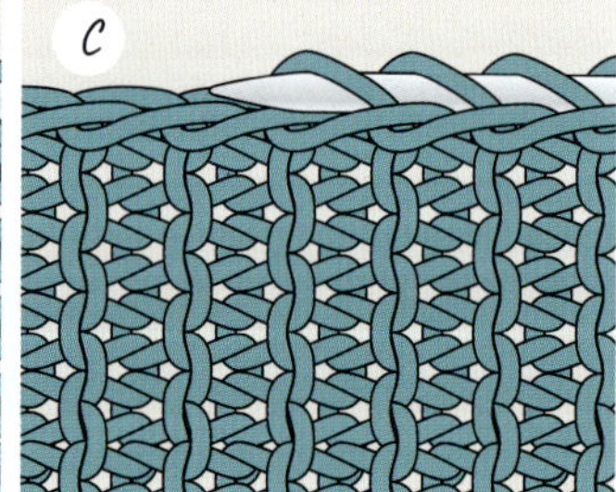

Picking up sts is not an exact science. In some cases you'll probably have to pick up sts in less obvious places to get the required number, e.g., in the corner knot of the cast-on edge.

Your first row is a RS row, so you need to slide the sts to the other end of the DPN.

**Row 1 (RS):** Knit.
**Rows 2–18:** Sl1p, k8.

Cast off.

If you want to continue with the same colour, you do not need to break the yarn, just put the skein through the last st, tighten the yarn and continue with the same ball of yarn.

### Section 3 (lower left rectangle)

Using a DPN, pick up 9 sts along the left edge of the square you just finished and 9 sts along the bottom of the first square you made. Notice that the bottom of the square is the cast-on edge, and here you only have a single row of legs, not a chain as you did along the sides. Pick up these legs.

**Row 1 (RS):** Knit.
**Rows 2–18:** Sl1p, k17.

Cast off.

### Section 4 (lower right rectangle):

Using a DPN, pick up 9 sts down the left edge of the section you just completed and 9 sts along the central square. The last 9 sts have the right leg in front of the needle, and are to be knitted the normal way **(C)**.

**Row 1 (RS):** Knit.
**Rows 2–18:** Sl1p, k17.

Cast off.

### Section 5 (top rectangle)

Using a DPN, pick up 9 sts along the left side of the section you just completed, 9 sts along the central square, and another 9 to complete the row. You should now have 27 sts in total.

**Row 1 (RS):** Knit.
**Rows 2–18:** Sl1p, k26.

Cast off and weave in ends.

### GEEKY NOTES 

In garter stitch, you can normally pick up one stitch per garter ridge along a perpendicular edge. In stocking stitch, a good ratio is to pick up five stitches every eight rows.

You may choose to pick up the front leg of the side chain, if you want a more seamless appearance. In this square, however, I wanted to accentuate the log cabin structure, so I placed the ridge formed by the front legs of the chains on the right-hand side.

If you find that you get large gaps and you want a tighter join, you can twist the stitches when knitting the first row.

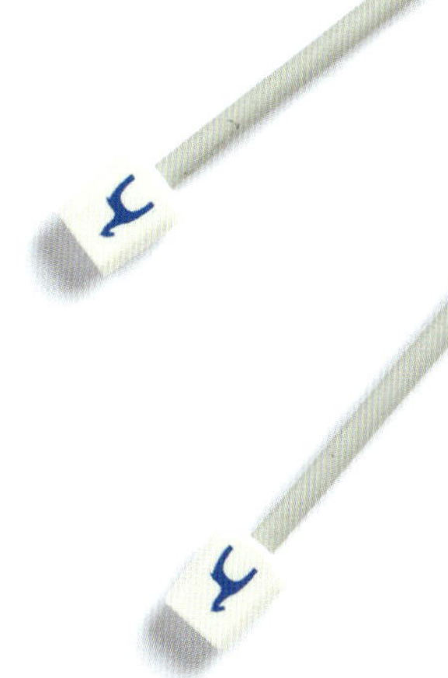

See clips 38.1, 38.2.

# 38. The Interlaced One

## *How to knit up stitches*

Entrelac is one of my favourite patterns. It's not as difficult as it looks, and it's even easier if you knit backwards instead of turning your knitting back and forth (see **30.** The Backwards One).

### YOU ALREADY KNOW HOW TO

- cast on, knit, and cast/bind off (**00**. The Basic One)
- slip the first stitch purlwise (**01**. The Slippy One)
- purl (**03**. The Purly One)
- follow a knitting pattern containing abbreviations (**04**. The Seedy One)
- decrease by knitting two stitches together (**06**. The Mitred One)
- place and slip a marker (**06**. The Mitred One)
- make a left-leaning decrease (**08**. The Left One)
- make a double decrease (**11**. The Convergent One)
- make twisted-loop increases (**13**. The Loopy One)
- work "make one" increases (**14**. The Neat One)
- make increases and decreases on purl rows (**15**. The Complicated One)
- knit in the round (**16**. The Circular One)
- slip the first stitch after a purl stitch (**26**. The Magic One)
- knit backwards (**30**. The Backwards One)
- pick up stitches (**37**. The Logged One)

EXTRA MATERIALS

- 5 DPNs or a pair of 40cm/16in circular needles
- a removable stitch marker

A

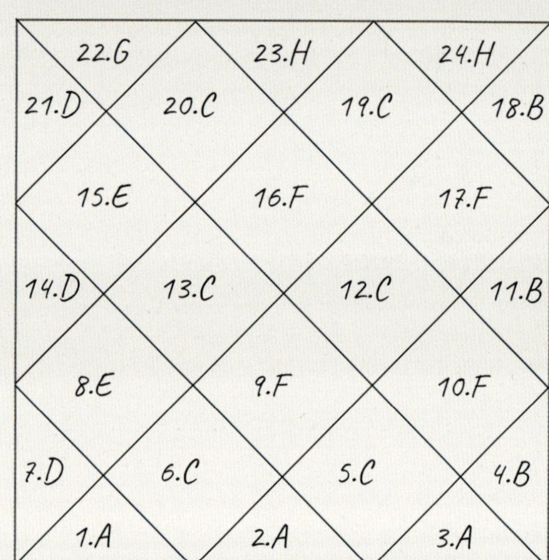

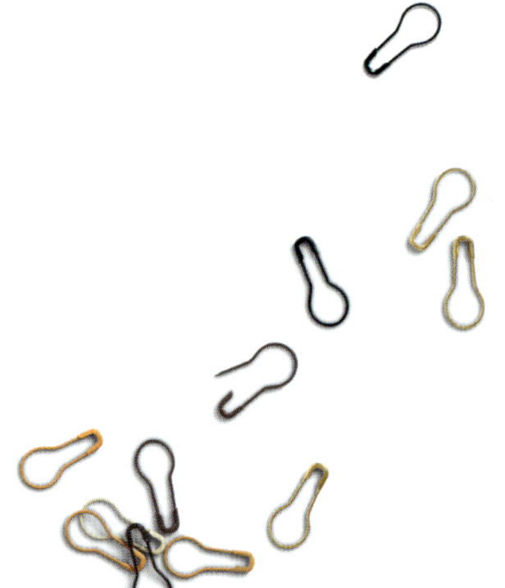

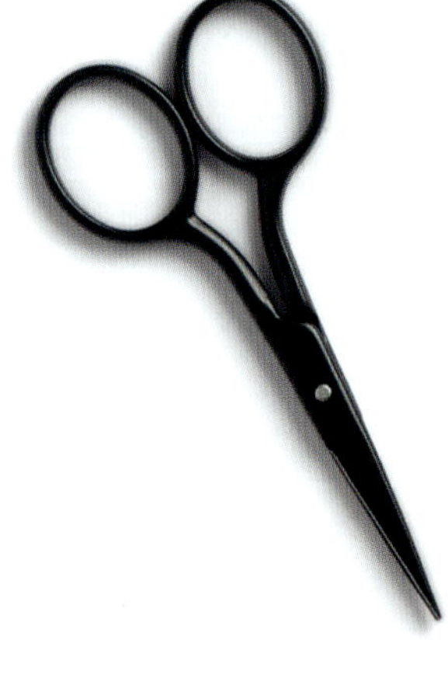

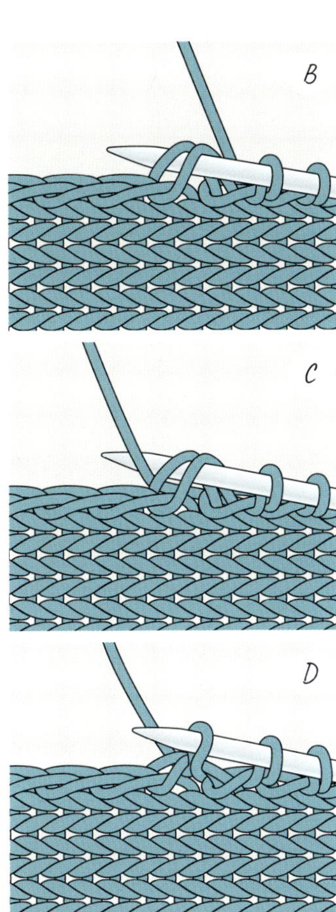


# Instructions

**(A)** shows the inner square, without the border. The numbers indicate the order in which you will knit the various sections, and the letters refer to the instructions you need to follow. Start by knitting triangle 1A at the lower left, following the instructions for Triangle A, followed by 2A and 3A. Next you will knit triangle 4B using the instructions for Triangle B, and so on.

You can choose to knit backwards instead of turning and purling.

Cast on 15 sts.

## Triangle A

**Row 1 (WS):** P1, turn.
**Row 2 (RS):** K1, turn.
**Row 3:** Sl1p, p1, turn.
**Row 4:** Sl1p, k1, turn.
**Row 5:** Sl1p, p2, turn.
**Row 6:** Sl1p, k2, turn.
**Row 7:** Sl1p, p3, turn.
**Row 8:** Sl1p, k3, turn.
**Row 9:** Sl1p, p4, do not turn.

Repeat Triangle A twice more. On the last row, turn and proceed to Triangle B.

## Triangle B

**Row 1 (RS):** K1, turn.
**Row 2 (WS):** P1, turn.
**Row 3:** Sl1p, k1, turn.
**Row 4:** Sl1p, p1, turn.

You will now start working SSKs, using one of the sts of the triangle (or square) below each time.

**Row 5:** Sl1p, M1L, SSK, turn.
**Row 6:** Sl1p, p2, turn.
**Row 7:** Sl1p, M1L, k1, SSK, turn.
**Row 8:** Sl1p, p3, turn.
**Row 9:** Sl1p, M1L, k2, SSK, do not turn.

Proceed to Square C.

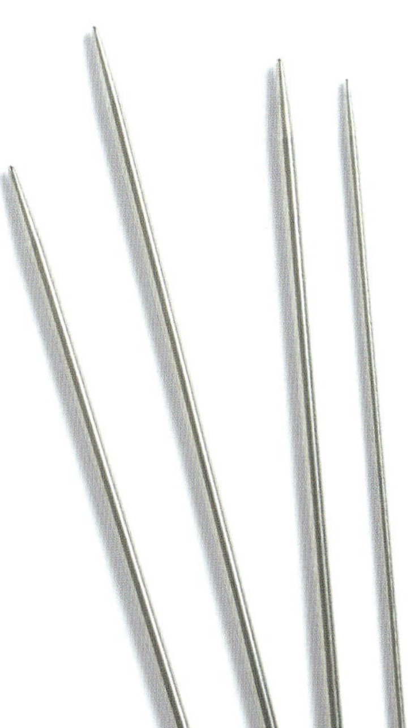

## Square C

You will now start knitting up sts.

**To knit up a st knitwise:** insert your needle into a selvedge st from front to back **(B)**, wrap the yarn around the needle tip **(C)** and pull it out again **(D)**, the same way you would knit a st off the LH needle.

**Row 1 (RS):** Knit up 5 sts along the edge of the triangle (or square) below, i.e., 1 st in each sl st and 1 more between the 2 triangles (or squares), turn.
**Row 2:** Sl1p, p4, turn.
**Row 3:** Sl1p, k3, SSK, turn.

Repeat Rows 2–3 until all the sts from the triangle (or square) below are knitted into the square, but do not turn on last row.

Repeat Square C once more. Proceed to Triangle D.

## Triangle D

**Row 1 (RS):** Knit up 5 sts knitwise along the left side of the triangle (or square) below (the last of these sts may be a bit tricky), turn.
**Row 2 (WS):** Sl1p, p4, turn.

Do not sl the st at the beginning of Row 3 – you'll need that when knitting up sts later!

**Row 3:** K3, k2tog, turn.
**Row 4:** Sl1p, p3, turn.
**Row 5:** Sl1p, k1, k2tog, turn.
**Row 6:** Sl1p, p2, turn.
**Row 7:** Sl1p, k2tog, turn.
**Row 8:** Sl1p, p1, turn.
**Row 9:** K2tog, turn.
**Row 10 (WS):** Sl1p, do not turn.

You should end with the WS of the work facing you, with 1 st on the RH needle and the rest of the sts in groups of 5 on the LH needle. Proceed to Square E.

## Square E

**Row 1 (WS):** You already have 1 st on your RH needle. Knit up 4 sts purlwise along the edge of the triangle you just finished, turn.

**To knit up a st purlwise:** insert the needle into a selvedge st from back to front **(E)**, wrap the yarn around the needle tip **(F)** and pull it out again **(G)**, the same way you would purl a st off the LH needle.

**Row 2:** Sl1p, k4, turn.
**Row 3:** Sl1p, p3, p2tog, turn.

Repeat Rows 2–3 until all the sts from the square below have been knitted into the square, but do not turn on last row. Proceed to Square F.

## Square F

**Row 1 (WS):** Use your RH needle to evenly pick up 5 sts purlwise along the edge of the square from the previous section, turn.

Work Rows 2–3 of Square E until all the sts from the square below have been knitted into the square, but do not turn on last row.

Repeat Square F once more. Turn.

Repeat Triangle B once, Square C twice and Triangle D once.

Repeat Square E once and Square F twice. Turn.

Repeat Triangle B once, Square C twice and Triangle D once.

Proceed to Triangle G.

## Triangle G

**Row 1 (WS):** You already have 1 st on your RH needle. Knit up 4 sts purlwise along the edge of the triangle (or square) below, turn.
**Row 2 (RS):** Sl1p, k4, turn.
**Row 3:** Sl1p, p3, k2tog, turn.
**Row 4:** Sl1p, k2, k2tog, turn.
**Row 5:** Sl1p, p2, p2tog, turn.
**Row 6:** Sl1p, k1, k2tog, turn.
**Row 7:** Sl1p, p1, p2tog, turn.
**Row 8:** Sl1p, k2tog, turn.
**Row 9:** Sl1p, p2tog, turn.
**Row 10:** K2tog, turn.
**Row 11:** P2tog, do not turn.

Proceed to Triangle H.

## Triangle H

**Row 1 (WS):** Knit up 5 sts purlwise along the edge of the square below, turn.
**Row 2 (RS):** Sl1p, k3, k2tog.

Work Rows 3–11 of Triangle G.
Repeat Triangle H.

Pass your skein through the last st to close it and continue without breaking the yarn.

## Border

Using a DPN, [knit up 5 sts along each triangle and 1 st between triangles (17 sts in total)] 4 times, using one DPN for each side. (68 sts)

Place a removable stitch marker at the beginning of the round. Continue knitting in the round and increase as follows:

**Rnd 1:** *K1, [make a twisted loop, k3] 5 times, make a twisted loop, k1.** Repeat from * to ** 4 times. (92 sts)

The twisted-loop increases will be hidden by the purl ridges in the next round, so you do not need to make them symmetrical.

**Rnd 2:** Purl.
**Rnd 3:** [K1, make twisted loop, k to last st on the needle, make twisted loop, k1] 4 times. (8 sts increased)
**Rnd 4:** Purl.
**Rnds 5–6:** Repeat Rnds 3–4 once more. (108 sts)

Cast off knitwise very loosely and weave in ends.

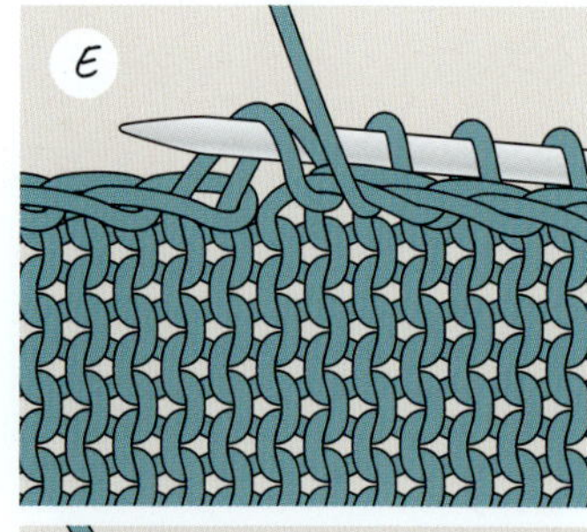


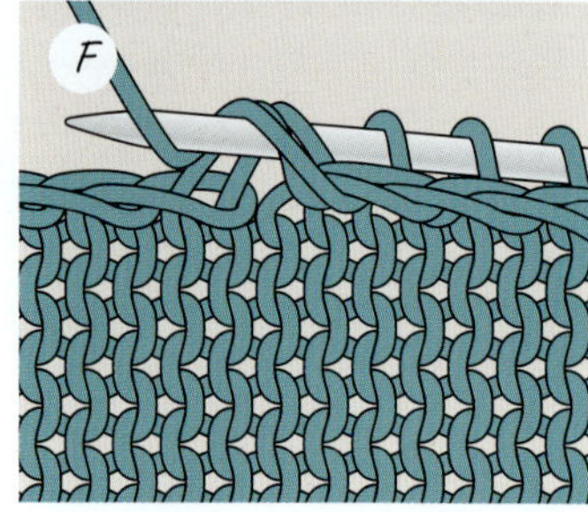


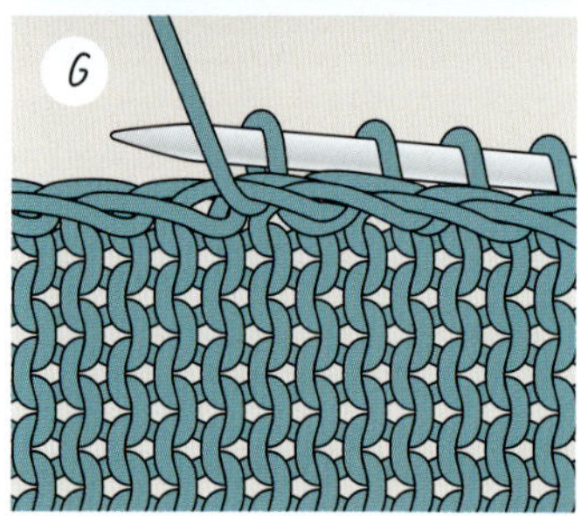


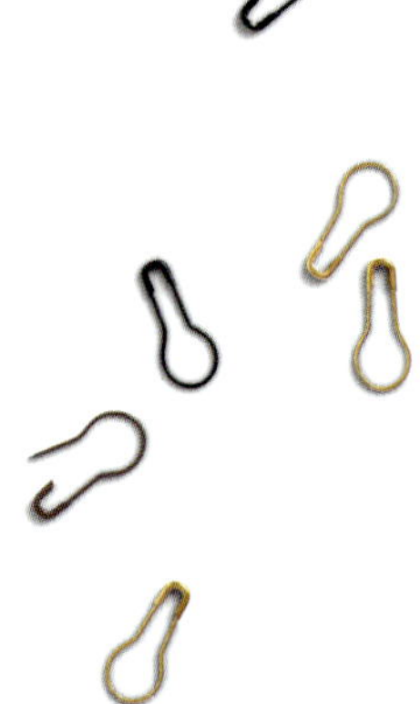

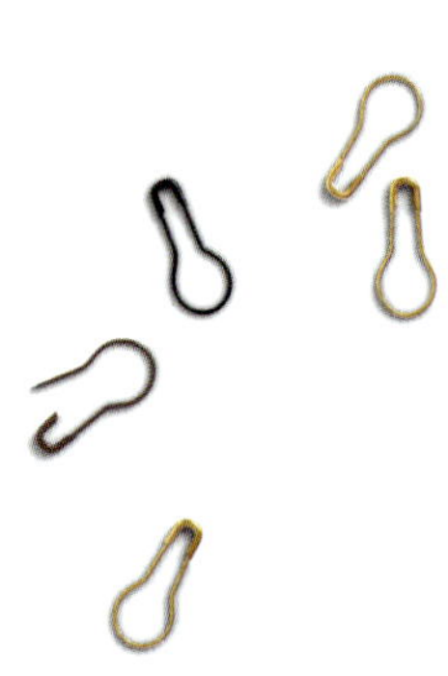

NOW YOU KNOW HOW TO
knit up stitches
work the entrelac pattern

# **39.** The Joined One

## *How to join knitted pieces with the three-needle cast off*

This square is knitted in two pieces which are then joined by knitting them together and casting off at the same time. This square may not look like much, but it's a very useful technique. I always use it when joining shoulder seams.

See clip 39.1.

### YOU ALREADY KNOW HOW TO

- cast on, knit, and cast/bind off (**00**. The Basic One)
- slip the first stitch purlwise (**01**. The Slippy One)
- follow a knitting pattern containing abbreviations (**04**. The Seedy One)
- decrease by knitting two stitches together (**06**. The Mitred One)

### EXTRA MATERIALS

- 3 DPNs
- yarn in 2 different colours

## Instructions

Using MC, cast on 27 sts.

**Rows 1–23:** Sl1p, k26.

You now have 12 garter ridges on the RS and your last row was a WS row. Leave the project aside.

Using CC, cast on 27 sts to another DPN.

**Rows 1–23:** Sl1p, k26.

**To work the three-needle cast-off:** place the 2 knitted pieces RS facing and with the knitting needles one behind the other. Use a third DPN and insert it knitwise into the first st of the front needle without slipping it off the needle, then insert it knitwise into the first st of the back needle **(A)** and knit these 2 sts together, slipping both of them off their respective needles **(B)**. Knit the second st of the front needle together with the second st of the back needle the same way. Sl the previous st over this last st **(C)**. Continue knitting 1 st from the front needle together with 1 st from the back needle and casting them off until you have cast off all the sts. Weave in the ends.

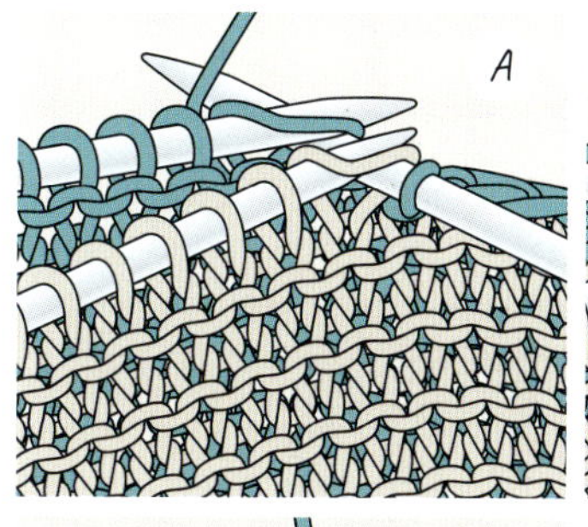


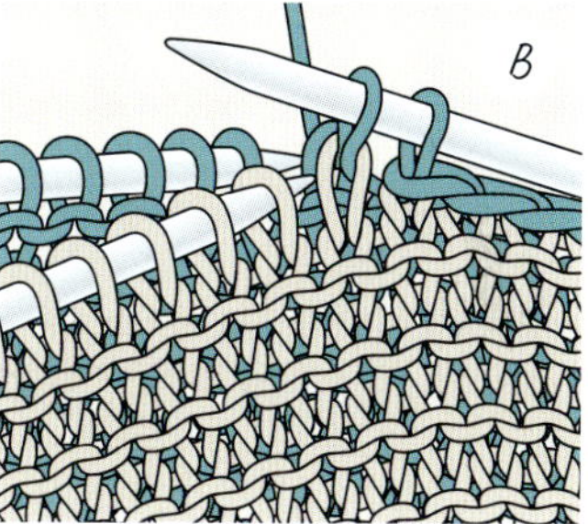


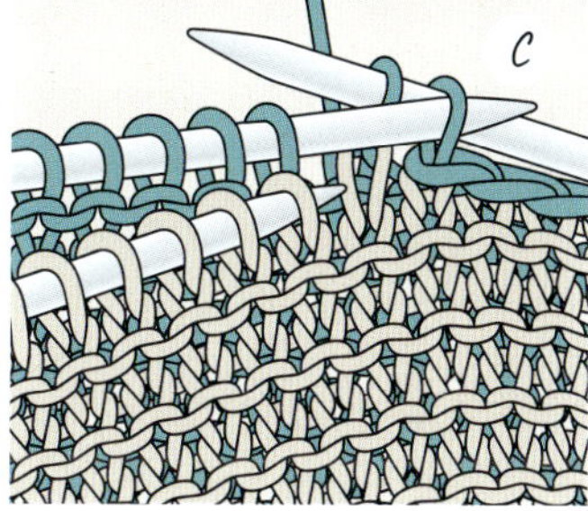


### GEEKY NOTES

Though there are more "invisible" ways of joining knitted pieces (such as grafting, see **41.** The Minimalist One), this method is very useful when you need a sturdy seam.

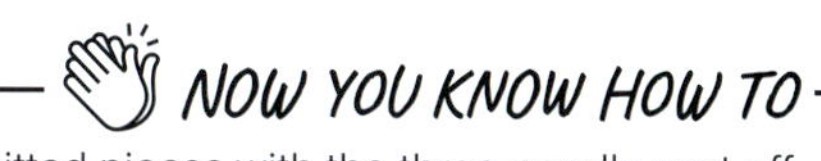

### NOW YOU KNOW HOW TO

join knitted pieces with the three-needle cast off

# **40.** The Pocketed One

### *How to join knitted pieces using the mattress stitch*

This square has a pocket, which you can use to keep your tissues, earplugs, or other small objects.

## YOU ALREADY KNOW HOW TO

- cast on, knit, and cast/bind off (**00**. The Basic One)
- slip the first stitch purlwise (**01**. The Slippy One)
- purl (**03**. The Purly One)
- follow a knitting pattern containing abbreviations (**04**. The Seedy One)
- make a kfb increase (**10**. The Diagonal One)
- make twisted-loop increases (**13**. The Loopy One)
- pick up stitches (**37**. The Logged One)

## EXTRA MATERIALS

- yarn in 2 different colours
- a DPN

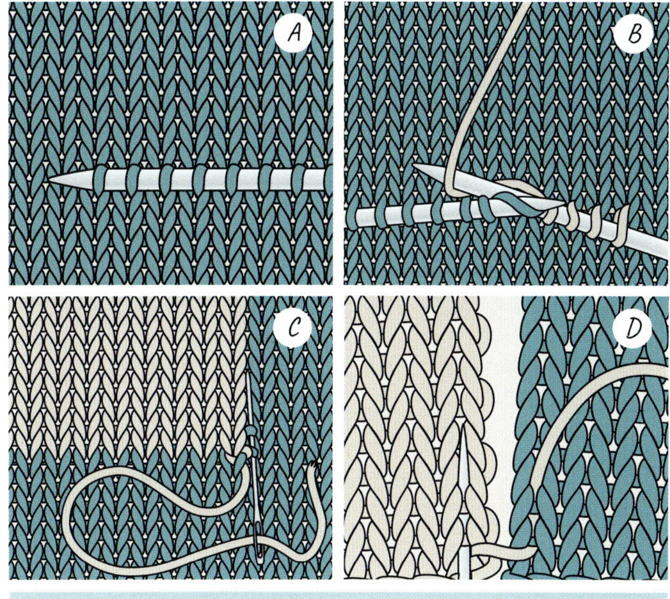

Anna's tips...

This way of picking up stitches can also be used to add a lifeline into your knit fabric if you need to undo a section of your knitting, as follows: pick up the right leg of each stitch in a row with circular needles thinner than the ones you have been knitting with. Check that all the stitches are in the same row. This is easy to see if you are knitting stripes or garter stitch. If you are knitting stocking stitch, check (or pick up the stitches on) the wrong side. Undo your knitting down to your lifeline and knit again using your regular needles.

## Instructions

Knit a square in stocking st with a garter-st border as in **03.** The Purly One.

**Make a pocket as follows:** using a DPN, pick up the right leg of each of the 13 centre sts of Row 11 of your square **(A)**. Check on the WS that the sts you picked up are all in the same row! Work the pocket using CC, leaving a 30cm/12in tail (which you will use to sew down the right side of the pocket.

**Row 1 (RS of pocket):** Starting on the RH side **(B)**, k12, kfb. (14 sts)
**Row 2:** (WS of pocket): Purl all sts, make a twisted loop. (15 sts)
**Row 3 (RS):** Knit.
**Row 4 (WS):** Purl.
**Rows 5–18:** Repeat Rows 3–4 another 7 times.
**Row 19 (RS):** As Row 3.
**Rows 20–24:** P1, k14.

Cast off. Break yarn, leaving a 30cm/12in tail, which you will use to sew down the LH side of the pocket.

Sew the sides of the pocket onto square using the mattress st, starting at the RH edge of the pocket.

To work mattress st: insert your tapestry needle between the 3rd and 4th knit st column from the border of the square, and move upwards picking 2 horizontal bars **(C)**. Next, insert it into the base of the pocket between the selvedge st and the second st and pick 2 horizontal bars, again moving upwards **(D)**. Now, insert the needle into the square fabric through the hole that it emerged from just before, picking up the 2 bars above. Insert the needle into the pocket and pick the next 2 bars. After a few sts, pull the yarn to tighten the st. Magic – you get a perfect join!

Continue in this way up to the top of the pocket.

Turn the square upside down to sew the left side of the pocket. Identify the row where you ended the pocket seam. This is best done on the WS of the square. Insert the needle here between the 3rd and 4th knit st column from the border and move upwards towards the base of the pocket.

Weave in ends.

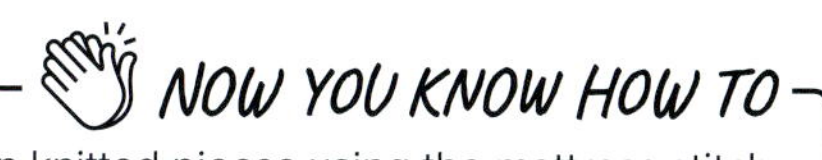

See clips 41.1, 41.2, 41.3, 41.4.

# 41. The Minimalist One

## *How to do the provisional cast on and how to graft knitted pieces together*

Sometimes you need to pick up stitches from the cast-on edge. You can do this completely seamlessly by using the provisional cast on. This gives you live stitches along the cast-on edge, which you can easily transfer onto a knitting needle.

### YOU ALREADY KNOW HOW TO

- cast on, knit, and cast/bind off (**00**. The Basic One)
- slip the first stitch purlwise (**01**. The Slippy One)
- purl (**03**. The Purly One)
- follow a knitting pattern containing abbreviations (**04**. The Seedy One)
- join knitted pieces with the three-needle cast off (**39**. The Joined One)

### EXTRA MATERIALS

- a crochet hook
- 3 DPNs
- 1m/40in of scrap yarn in a contrasting colour
- 1m/40in of CC yarn

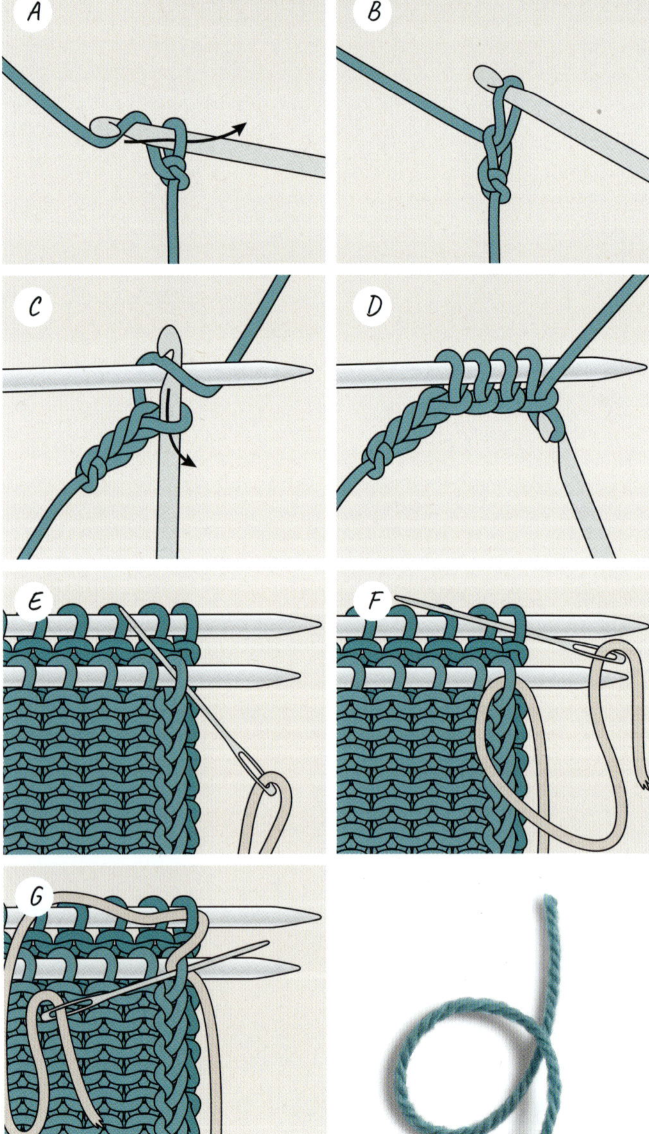

## Instructions

### First half

Using MC, cast on 27 sts.

**Rows 1–6:** Sl1p, k26.
**Row 7 (WS):** Sl1p, k3, p19, k4.
**Row 8 (RS):** Sl1p, k26.
**Rows 9–24:** Repeat rows 7–8 another 8 times.

You should now have 12 garter ridges in the garter-st border. Lay aside and restart on another needle.

### Second half

Using a length of scrap yarn approx 1m/40in long and preferably in a contrasting colour, cast on 27 sts with the provisional cast on method using a crochet hook.

To work the provisional cast on: make a slip knot, make 3 chain sts as follows: bring the yarn over the hook (like a yarn over), catch it with the hook **(A)**, and draw it through the st **(B)**. Place the knitting needle behind the crochet hook, wrap the yarn around both needles **(C)**, pull it through with the crochet hook as if making a chain st, thus making a loop on the knitting needle **(D)**. Repeat until you have 27 sts on the knitting needle. Make another 3 chain sts and pull the yarn through the last st to close the st.

Continue with MC.

**Row 1 (WS):** K27.
**Row 2 (RS):** Sl1p, k26.
**Row 3 (WS):** Sl1p, k3, p19, k4.
**Rows 4–17:** Repeat Rows 2 and 3 another 7 times.
**Rows 18–23:** Sl1p, k26.

Cast off.

Undo the last st of the chain. Unravel the chain sts one by one and transfer the exposed sts onto a DPN. Notice that on this piece you only have 26 sts!

Now hold the 2 pieces with WS together, with the first half in front. Use a tapestry needle and approx 1m/40in of CC yarn to graft the 2 pieces together. The first and last 4 sts are to be worked in garter st, while the central 19 sts are to be worked in stocking st, which is the kind of grafting used most often.

**To graft in garter st:** enter the first st on the front needle purlwise **(E)** leaving it on the knitting needle and draw the yarn through leaving a 10cm/4in tail, which you will weave in afterwards. Enter the first st on the back needle purlwise **(F)** leaving it on the knitting needle. Enter the front st knitwise **(G)** and slip it off the needle. Draw the yarn snug, but not tight. Tension is key! You want the sts to have the same height as your knitted sts. *Enter the next st on the front needle purlwise. Enter the back st knitwise and slip it off the needle. Enter the next st on the back needle purlwise. Enter the front st knitwise and slip it off the needle** to the end of the garter st border (i.e., 3 times). Think: purl(wise), knit(wise) off, purl(wise), knit(wise) off.

You have now reached the stocking st section.

**To graft in stocking st:** ***enter the next st on the front needle purlwise. Enter the back st purlwise and slip it off the needle. Enter the next st on the back needle knitwise. Enter the front st knitwise and slip it off the needle****, repeat from *** to **** until you reach the garter-st border. Think: "purl(wise), purl(wise) off, knit(wise), knit(wise) off".

Now repeat your garter-st graft from * to ** until the end (i.e., 3 times).

**To finish:** Enter the next st on the front needle purlwise. Enter the back st knitwise and slip it off the needle. Enter the st on the back needle purlwise. Slip the last st off the needle and weave in the ends.

This square may not look like much, but you and I both know that you've just mastered two very cool techniques.

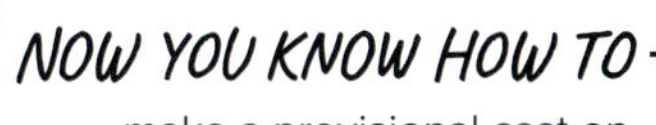


make a provisional cast on
graft knitted pieces together
make a crochet chain

See clip 42.1.

# 42. The Short One

## *How to knit German short rows*

Short rows are used to shape your knits. They are made by turning your knitting before reaching the end of a row, which will create a hole at the turning point. Several short-row techniques exist that avoid creating this hole. My preferred technique is German short rows.

### YOU ALREADY KNOW HOW TO

- cast on, knit, and cast/bind off (**00**. The Basic One)
- slip the first stitch purlwise (**01**. The Slippy One
- knit horizontal stripes (**02**. The Striped One)
- follow a knitting pattern containing abbreviations (**04**. The Seedy One)
- decrease by knitting two stitches together (**06**. The Mitred One)
- make a yarn over (**07**. The Holey One)
- knit backwards (**30**. The Backwards One)

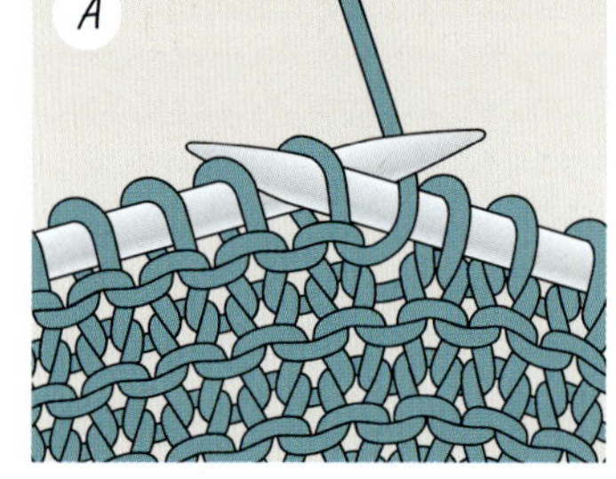


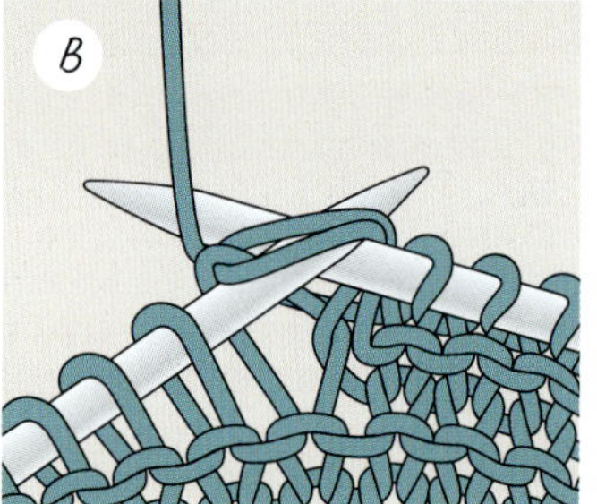


### NEW ABBREVIATIONS

**DS:** double stitch

### EXTRA MATERIALS

- yarn in 2 different colours

## Instructions

Using MC, cast on 27 sts.

**Rows 1–6:** Sl1p, k26.
**Row 7 (WS):** Sl1p, k11, turn (do not complete the row).

On the first short row, you will make a double stitch (DS).

**To make a DS:** slip the next st (the "pivot" st) purlwise without bringing the yarn in front **(A)**. This is the equivalent of a sl st and a YO. In practice, it is done in one movement and the result looks like 2 sts. Make sure to pull the yarn to get a tight pivot stitch, otherwise, you will have a hole.

**SR1:** DS, knit to end of row.
**SR2:** Sl1p, k10, turn.
**SR3:** DS, knit to end of row.
**SR4:** Sl1p, k9 (i.e., knit to DS, do not knit DS), turn.
**SR5:** DS, knit to end of row.

Continue this way, knitting to the DS then turning on WS rows, and knitting to the end of the row on RS rows, until:

**SR12:** Sl1p, k5, turn.
**SR13:** DS, knit to end of row.
At this point, you should have 10 garter ridges on the LH side of the work when looking at the RS.

**Row 8 (WS):** Sl1p, k26, knitting each DS as if it were a single stitch **(B)** throughout this square.
**Row 9 (RS):** Sl1p, k11, turn.

Repeat SR1–SR13. At this point, you should have 11 garter ridges on each side of the work, but not in the middle, when looking at the RS.

Continue with CC.

**Rows 10–11:** Sl1p, k26.
Continue with MC.

**Row 12 (RS):** Sl1p, k15, turn.

**SR14:** DS, k4, turn.
**SR15:** DS, k5 (i.e., k to DS, k DS as a single st, k1), turn.

Continue this way, knitting 1 st past the DS on every row, until:

**SR26:** DS, k16, turn.
**SR27:** DS, k to end of row, turn.
**SR28:** Sl1p, k22, turn.
**SR29:** DS, k18, turn.
**SR30:** DS, k17 (i.e., k to DS, do not k DS), turn.

Continue this way, knitting to the DS then turning on every row until:

**SR41:** DS, k6, turn.
**SR42:** DS, k to end of row.

Continue with CC.

**Rows 13–14:** Sl1p, k26.

Continue with MC.

**Row 15 (RS):** Sl1p, k5, turn.
**SR43:** DS, k to end of row.
**SR44:** Sl1p, k6 (i.e., k to DS, k DS as a single st, k1), turn.
**SR45:** DS, k to end of row.

Continue this way, knitting 1 st past the DS on RS rows and knitting to the end of the row on WS rows, until:

**SR54:** Sl1p, k11, turn.
**SR55:** DS, k to end of row.
**Row 16 (RS):** Sl1p, k26.
**Row 17 (WS):** Sl1p, k5, turn.

Repeat SR43–SR55.

**Rows 18–22:** Sl1p, k26.

Cast off and weave in ends.

## GEEKY NOTES

No matter whether you are knitting garter stitch or stocking stitch, or whether you are on the right or the wrong side, the double stitch is worked in the same way. There are many ways of working short rows. Here are some of them:

- Turn, slip the first stitch, pull the yarn a bit to get a tight stitch at the turning point, and knit on. This method may produce a gap, which is why the next three methods were invented.
- Wrap-and-turn short rows: knit to the pivot stitch, slip the stitch, wrap the yarn around it, slip it back again, turn the work and knit back. Next time you get to that stitch, lift the wrap onto the left-hand needle and knit it together with the yarn you wrapped around it.
- Japanese short rows: knit to the pivot stitch, place a removable marker on the working yarn and knit the pivot stitch. Turn, slip the pivot stitch and knit on. When you need to knit the pivot stitch, lift the yarn with the marker onto the left-hand needle, remove the marker and knit the stitch together with this yarn.

Even though wrap-and-turn short rows and Japanese short rows produce a neat result, I find that German short rows are a lot easier and produce an equally good result.

If your short rows are really short, you can knit backwards instead of turning the work back and forth.

See clips 43.1, 43.2, 43.3.

# 43. The Lifted One

### *How to work the pinhole cast on and make lifted increases*

This square is knit in the round from the centre towards the edge using the pinhole cast on. It also introduces lifted increases, a good alternative to "make one" increases if you need neat symmetrical increases in stocking stitch.

## YOU ALREADY KNOW HOW TO

- cast on, knit, and cast/bind off (**00**. The Basic One)
- purl (**03**. The Purly One)
- follow a knitting pattern containing abbreviations (**04**. The Seedy One)
- place and slip a marker (**06**. The Mitred One)
- knit in the round (**16**. The Circular One)

## EXTRA MATERIALS

- 5 DPNs
- a removable stitch marker

## NEW ABBREVIATIONS

**LLI:** left lifted increase
**RLI:** right lifted increase

## Instructions

Using a DPN, cast on 12 sts with the pinhole cast on.

**To make the pinhole cast-on:** wind a length of yarn around the 3 middle fingers of your left hand **(A)**. Hold the tail at the back and anchor it between your ring and little fingers. Take a DPN and make a YO with the working yarn (the yarn bottom left connected to the ball) **(B)**. This is your first st. Now go behind the loop on your hand and pick the working yarn **(C)**. This is your second st **(D)**. Continue these 2 motions until you have 12 sts in total **(E)**. By pulling the tail, you can tighten the hole **(F)**, but you do not need to close it completely just yet.

Slide the sts to the other end of the DPN and start knitting. For the first couple of rounds, it's easier to work with 2 needles. Eventually you will distribute the sts equally on 4 DPNs **(G)**.

**Rnd 1:** [P1, k1, p1] twice, using another DPN [p1, k1, p1] twice.

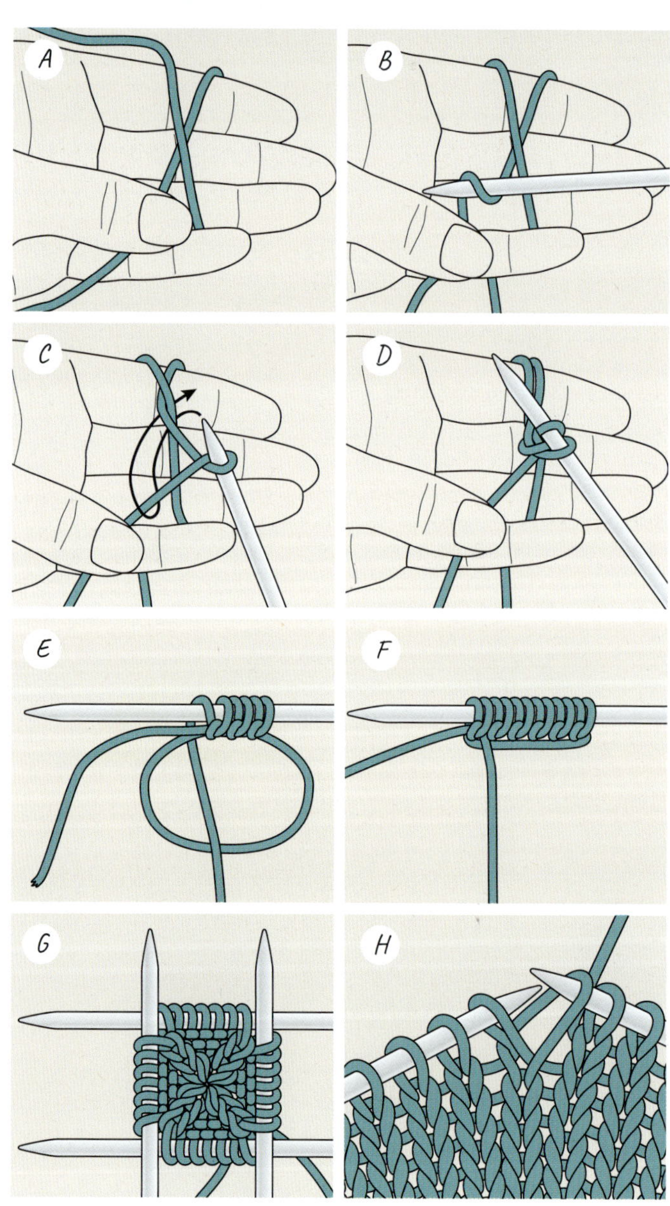

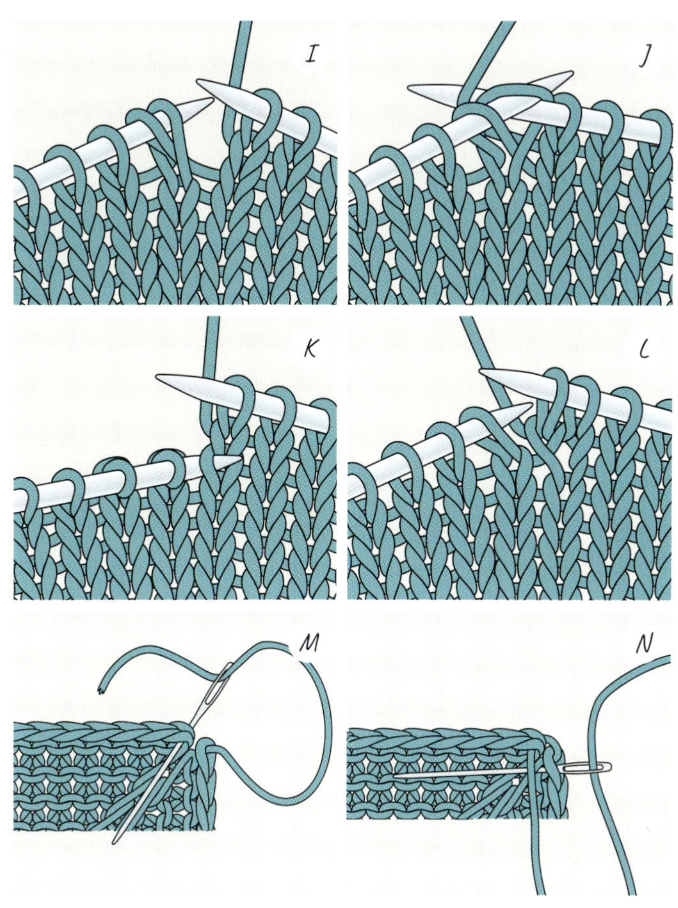


You now have 12 sts distributed on 2 needles, 6 sts on each needle. Mark the beginning of the round with a removable marker or a piece of scrap yarn.

**Rnd 2:** [P1, RLI, k1, LLI, p1] 4 times. (20 sts)

**To make a RLI:** using your RH needle, pick the right leg of the st below the st on your LH needle **(H)**, lift it onto your LH needle **(I)** and knit it **(J)**. Continue by knitting (or purling) the st on the LH needle as you normally would.

**To make a LLI:** using your LH needle, pick the left leg of the st 2 sts below the st on your RH needle **(K)** and knit it through the back loop **(L)**.

At this stage, it's still a bit tricky to identify the legs of the st you need to lift for the increases. It will be a lot easier from now on.

On Rnd 3, distribute the sts onto 4 DPNs, 5 sts on each needle.

**Rnd 3:** [P1, k3, p1] 4 times.
**Rnd 4:** [P1, RLI, k to 1 st before end of needle, LLI, p1] 4 times. (8 sts increased)
**Rnd 5:** [P1, k to 1 st before end of needle, p1] 4 times.
**Rnds 6–9:** Repeat Rnds 4–5 twice more. (52 sts)
**Rnd 10:** As Rnd 4. (8 sts increased)
**Rnd 11:** As Rnd 5.
**Rnd 12:** [P1, RLI, p to 1 st before end of needle, LLI, p1] 4 times. (60 sts)

Even though this is a purl row, the increases are lifted from a knit row and are knitted, not purled, so they are worked exactly as before.

**Rnds 13–24:** Repeat Rnds 11–12 another 6 times. (108 sts)

As you increase, you may want to transfer your sts to circular needles. If you do so, remember to place a marker for the beginning of the round and at every needle change.

Cast off knitwise very loosely. I use a 5mm needle (US size 8 or UK size 6), for this. Pull the cast-on tail to tighten the hole. Weave in ends. When weaving in the last end, close the gap by completing the chain formed around the square **(M, N)**.

## GEEKY NOTES 

**Why is the LLI lifted from a stitch two rows below?**

Because the stitch in question has already been knitted, while in the RLI it's only knitted after you lift it.

 *NOW YOU KNOW HOW TO*

work the pinhole cast on
make lifted increases

See clips 44.1, 44.2.

# 44. The Really Nerdy One

## *How to make symmetrical and double kfb increases*

The mirrored kfb and the kfb double increases are not widely used, so this is a rather nerdy square. For the geeks out there, I thought it might be interesting to explore the structure and the derivatives of this increase.

### YOU ALREADY KNOW HOW TO

- cast on, knit, and cast/bind off (**00**. The Basic One)
- purl (**03**. The Purly One)
- follow a knitting pattern containing abbreviations (**04**. The Seedy One)
- decrease by knitting two stitches together (**06**. The Mitred One)
- place and slip a marker (**06**. The Mitred One)
- make a left-leaning decrease (**08**. The Left One)
- make a double decrease (**11**. The Convergent One)
- knit in the round (**16**. The Circular One)
- knit backwards (**30**. The Backwards One)
- make bobbles (**30**. The Backwards One)
- close the gap next to a bobble (**31**. The Knobbly One)
- do the pinhole cast on (**43**. The Lifted One)

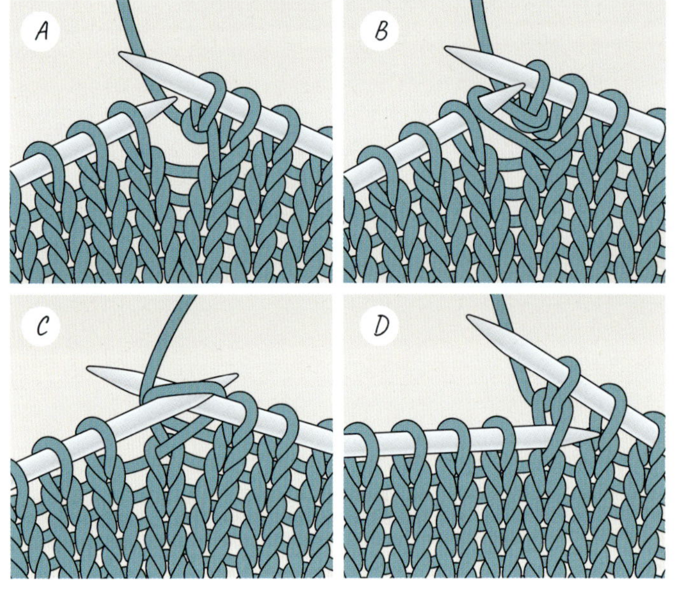


### EXTRA MATERIALS

- 5 DPNs
- a removable stitch marker

## Instructions

Using a DPN, cast on 12 sts with the pinhole cast on. Slide the sts to the other end of the needle and begin knitting with another DPN.

**Rnd 1:** *[K1, make double increase, k1] twice.** Continue with another dpn. Repeat from * to **. (20 sts)

**To make this double increase:** k the st through the back loop, then through the front loop before slipping it off the needle **(A)**. Lastly, with your LH needle, pick the vertical strand between the 2 sts **(B)** and k a st through this loop.

**Rnd 2:** [K1, p3, k1] 4 times.

On Rnd 3, transfer your sts onto 4 DPNs.

**Rnd 3:** [Kfb, k3, mirrored kfb, change needle] 4 times. (28 sts)

**To make a mirrored kfb:** change the mount of the st, i.e. place it with the left leg in front of the needle, knit the st through the front leg, which means you will twist the st but in the opposite direction of a st worked through the back loop **(C)**. Now, with your LH needle, pick the front leg of the st you just knitted **(D)** and knit a st through this loop.

Mark the beginning of the round with a removable marker.

**Rnd 4:** [K1, p 5, k1] 4 times.
**Rnd 5:** [Kfb, k5, mirrored kfb] 4 times. (36 sts)

**Rnd 6:** [K1, p7, k1] 4 times.
**Rnd 7:** [Kfb, k7, mirrored kfb] 4 times. (44 sts)

**Rnd 8:** [K1, p4, make bobble, p4, k1] 4 times.

**To make a bobble:** make a double increase as described above, turn, p3 (or knit backwards), turn, CDD.

**Rnd 9:** [Kfb, k9, mirrored kfb] 4 times, closing the gap before each bobble as in **31.** The Knobbly One. (52 sts)
**Rnd 10:** [K1, p4, make bobble, p1, make bobble, p4, k1] 4 times.
**Rnd 11:** [Kfb, k11, mirrored kfb] 4 times, closing the bobble gaps. (60 sts)
**Rnd 12:** [K1, p6, make bobble, p6, k1] 4 times.
**Rnd 13:** [Kfb, k13, mirrored kfb] 4 times, closing the bobble gaps. (68 sts)
**Rnd 14:** [K1, p to st before end of needle, k1] 4 times.
**Rnd 15:** [Kfb, k to st before end of needle, mirrored kfb] 4 times. (8 sts increased)
**Rnds 16–23:** Repeat Rnds 14-15 another 5 times (108 sts).

Cast off knitwise very loosely. Pull the cast-on tail to tighten the hole. Weave in ends.

**NOW YOU KNOW HOW TO**

make symmetrical and double kfb increases

# 45. The Bamboo One

## *How to work the bamboo stitch*

The next three patterns are produced using long strands between stitches. First up: bamboo stitch, which makes use of yarn overs to bind pairs of stitches together, imitating the shape of bamboo stems.

 YOU ALREADY KNOW HOW TO

- cast on, knit, and cast/bind off (**00.** The Basic One)
- slip the first stitch purlwise (**01.** The Slippy One)
- purl (**03.** The Purly One)
- follow a knitting pattern containing abbreviations (**04.** The Seedy One)
- decrease by knitting two stitches together (**06.** The Mitred One)
- make a yarn over (**07.** The Holey One)
- work "make one" increases (**14.** The Neat One)

## Instructions

Cast on 27 sts.

**Rows 1–4:** Sl1p, k26.
**Row 5 (WS):** Sl1p, k12, M1L, k14. (28 sts)
**Row 6 (RS):** Sl1p, k3, [YO, k2, pass the YO over the 2 sts] 10 times, k4.
**Row 7 (WS):** Sl1p, k3, p19, k4.
**Rows 8–41:** Repeat Rows 6–7 another 17 times.
**Row 42 (RS):** Sl1p, k11, k2tog, k14. (27 sts)
**Rows 43–47:** Sl1p, k26.

Cast off knitwise.

That's all there is to it!

work the bamboo stitch

# 46. The Blooming One

### *How to work the dandelion stitch*

The dandelion stitch is worked by pulling long loops through a stitch a few rows below.

## *YOU ALREADY KNOW HOW TO*

- cast on, knit, and cast/bind off (**00**. The Basic One)
- slip the first stitch purlwise (**01**. The Slippy One)
- purl (**03**. The Purly One)
- follow a knitting pattern containing abbreviations (**04**. The Seedy One)
- make a double increase (**12**. The Budding One)
- make increases and decreases on purl rows (**15**. The Complicated One)

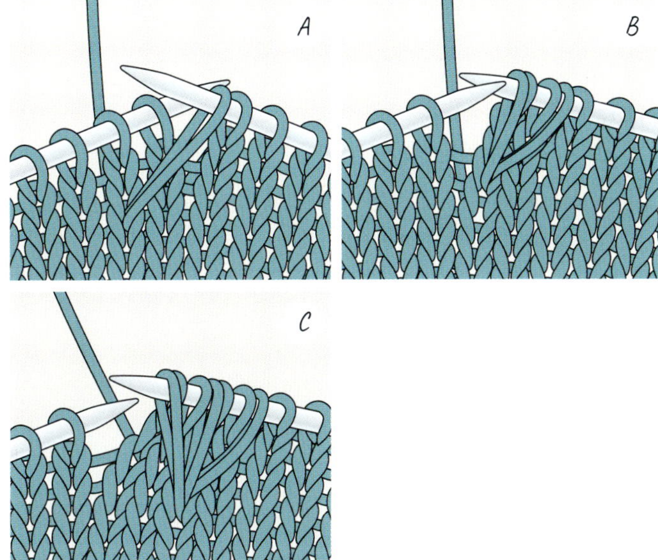


## Instructions

Using MC, cast on 27 sts.

**Rows 1–6:** Sl1p, k26.
**Row 7 (WS):** Sl1p, k3, p19, k4.
**Row 8 (RS):** Sl1p, k26.
**Rows 9–10:** Repeat Rows 7–8 once more.
**Row 11 (WS):** As Row 7.
**Row 12 (RS):** Sl1p, k6, make flower, k6, make flower, k6.

**To make a flower:** insert RH needle into the second st on the LH needle 3 rows down (this will be the centre of the flower) and draw up a loop **(A)**. Leave the loop on the RH needle and k2, make another loop into the same st **(B)**, k2, make a third loop into the same st **(C)**. Make sure that your loops are loose enough to lie flat.

**Row 13 (WS):** Sl1p, k3, p2, p2tog (i.e., purl the long loop together with the following st), [p1, p2tog] twice, p5, p2tog, [p1, p2tog] twice, p2, k4.
**Row 14 (RS):** Sl1p, k26.
**Row 15 (WS):** Sl1p, k3, p19, k4.
**Rows 16–23:** Repeat Rows 14–15 another 4 times.
**Row 24 (RS):** Sl1p, k11, make flower, k to end of row.
**Row 25 (WS):** Sl1p, k3, p7, [p2tog, p1] twice, p2tog, p7, k4.
**Row 26–35:** Repeat Rows 14–15 another 5 times.
**Rows 36–37:** Repeat Rows 12–13 once more.
**Row 38–41:** Repeat Rows 14–15 twice more.
**Rows 42–47:** Sl1p, k26.

Cast off and weave in ends.

## GEEKY NOTES

If you are knitting in the round, the loops are knitted together with the previous stitch in the next round.

# 47. The Royal One

## *How to work the Royal Quilt pattern*

This pattern is a variation on mosaic knitting. Some of the strands are passed in front of the knitting, instead of behind, and are caught in a subsequent row, producing this amazing pattern, known as the Royal Quilt.

 YOU ALREADY KNOW HOW TO

- cast on, knit, and cast/bind off (**00**. The Basic One)
- slip the first stitch purlwise (**01**. The Slippy One)
- knit horizontal stripes (**02**. The Striped One)
- purl (**03**. The Purly One)
- follow a knitting pattern containing abbreviations (**04**. The Seedy One)
- decrease by knitting two stitches together (**06**. The Mitred One)
- knit stranded colourwork on two needles (**22**. The Flat One)
- work the mosaic technique (**24**. The Mosaic One)

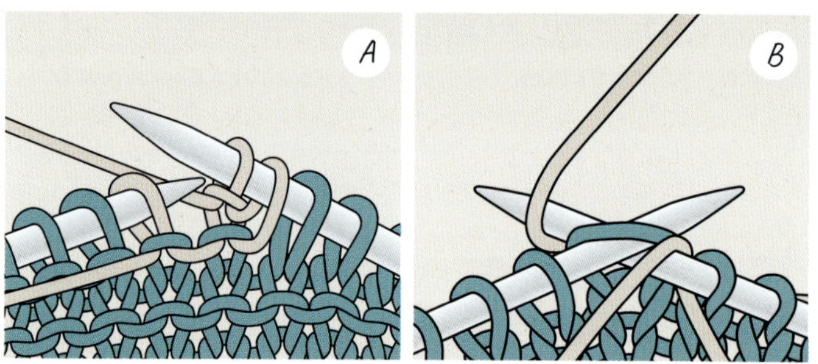

## Instructions

Using MC, cast on 27 sts.

**Rows 1–15:** Sl1p, k26.
**Row 16 (RS):** Sl1p, k5, change to CC, k2, sl5p wyib, k1, sl5p wyib, k2, turn.

**SR1:** YO, p2, sl5p wyib, p1, sl5p wyib, p2, leave CC hanging on the WS, turn.

It is not very common to have a yarn over at the beginning of a row **(A)**.

**SR2:** Change to MC, sl1p wyib, k13, sl1p wyib, k2tog (the st and the YO), k5.

Make the floats loose, especially the ones on the RS, as you will be pulling them up later.

**Row 17 (WS):** Sl1p, k4, p1, sl1p wyif, p13, sl1p wyif, p1, using CC make a reverse YO and leave the yarn hanging in front (the WS), k5 MC.
**Row 18 (RS):** Sl1p, k4, k2tog (the st and the YO), drop MC and continue with CC, k1, sl3p wyib, pick up the CC float with your RH needle **(B)** and k it together with the next st, sl5p wyib, k float together with the next st, sl3p wyib, k1, turn.

**SR1:** YO, p1, sl3p wyib, p1, sl5p wyib, p1, sl3p wyib, p1, leave CC hanging on the WS, turn.
**SR2:** Change to MC, sl1p wyib, k13, sl1p wyib, k2tog, k5.

**Row 19 (WS):** As Row 17.
**Row 20 (RS):** Sl1p, k4, k2tog, drop MC and continue with CC, k1, [k float together with the next st, sl5p wyib] twice, k float together with the next st, k1, turn.

**SR1:** YO, p2, sl5p wyib, p1, sl5p wyib, p2, leave CC hanging on the WS, turn.
**SR2:** Change to MC, sl1p wyib, k13, sl1p wyib, k2tog, k5.

**Row 21 (WS):** As Row 17.
**Rows 22–29:** Repeat Rows 18–21 twice more.
**Rows 30–31:** Repeat Rows 18–19 once more.

You should now have 16 purl ridges on the border.

**Row 32 (RS):** Sl1p, k4, k2tog, drop MC and continue with CC, k1, [k float together with the next st, sl5p wyib] twice, k float together with the next st, k1, turn

**SR1:** YO, p2, sl5p wyif (in front, not in the back as on Row 20), p1, sl5p wyif, p2, break CC, turn and continue with MC.
**SR2:** K15, k2tog, k5.

**Rows 33–47:** Sl1p, k26.

Cast off and weave in ends.

## GEEKY NOTES 

### Why the yarn over at the beginning of the row?

When knitting colourwork flat, the challenge is to get the first and last stitches of the new colour neat and tidy, because both legs of these stitches point in the same direction. To remedy this, you can bring up the yarn before knitting the first stitch, hence the yarn over. This same principle was used in **17.** The Jogless One, **22.** The Flat one, and **23.** The Difficult One.

NOW YOU KNOW HOW TO
work the Royal Quilt stitch

See clip 48.1.

# 48. The Squishy One

## *How to knit brioche*

Brioche knitting has a squishy, luscious texture and is fully reversible, so it is very well suited for scarves. One-colour brioche is an easy stitch, but it is difficult to combine with other kinds of knitting because it is much thicker, and has a much higher row count than plain knitting. This is why this square is to be joined sideways to the others.

### YOU ALREADY KNOW HOW TO

- cast on, knit, and cast/bind off (**00**. The Basic One)
- slip the first stitch purlwise (**01**. The Slippy One)
- follow a knitting pattern containing abbreviations (**04**. The Seedy One)
- decrease by knitting two stitches together (**06**. The Mitred One)
- make a yarn over (**07**. The Holey One)

### NEW ABBREVIATIONS

Two main stitches make up brioche knitting:

**brk:** brioche knit, i.e., knit a stitch together with its yarn over
**sl1yo:** slip one stitch purlwise + yarn over

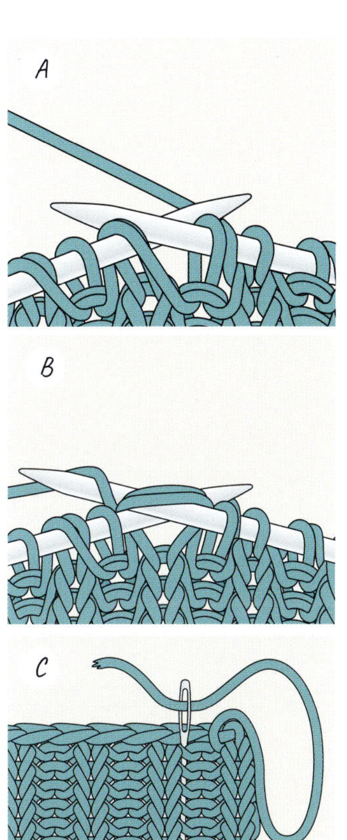


## Instructions

Cast on 25 sts.

**Row 1 (WS):** Sl1p, [sl1yo, k1] to end of row.

**To make a sl1yo:** go behind the working yarn and sl the st purlwise. Freeze!! Do not bring the yarn in front, just leave it lying over the RH needle **(A)**.

**Row 2 (RS):** Sl1p, [brk, sl1yo] to last 2 sts, brk, k1.

**To make a brk:** knit the st together with its YO **(B)**.

**Row 3 (WS):** Sl1p, [sl1yo, brk] to last 2 sts, sl1yo, k1.
**Rows 4–57:** Repeat Rows 2–3 another 27 times.

Cast off very loosely and weave in ends.

In brioche, the ends can be woven into the channel next to each knit st between the 2 layers of yarn **(C)**.

Because of its shape, this square is to be joined sideways to the others, i.e., you should join the cast-on edge to the side of one of the other squares.

### If you are a thrower...

Rules for the yarn over apply, i.e., the yarn needs to be in front before you do a sl1yo.

**To make a sl1yo:** bring the yarn to front, sl the st, then brk the next st without changing the position of the yarn. That way you will get a yarn over.

### GEEKY NOTES 

There are two ways of working this pattern. I use the one described above. The other way is: k1, k1 below, i.e., you put the needle through the stitch underneath the stitch on your LH needle and knit that stitch. That way, you get a stitch and a yarn over on your RH needle. This is often referred to as Fisherman's rib, though the result is structurally the same as brioche.

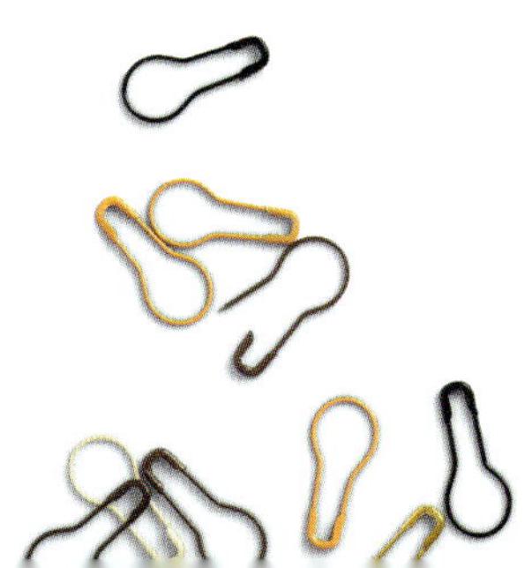

See clips 49.1, 49.2.

# **49.** The Accented One

## *How to knit two-colour brioche*

Brioche can also be worked in two colours, accenting the lovely structure of this stitch. To work this pattern, you will also need to use the brioche purl stitch.

### YOU ALREADY KNOW HOW TO

- cast on, knit, and cast/bind off (**00**. The Basic One)
- slip the first stitch purlwise (**01**. The Slippy One)
- purl (**03**. The Purly One)
- follow a knitting pattern containing abbreviations (**04**. The Seedy One)
- decrease by knitting two stitches together (**06**. The Mitred One)
- make a yarn over (**07**. The Holey One)
- make increases and decreases on purl rows (**15**. The Complicated One)
- knit brioche (**48**. The Squishy One)

### EXTRA MATERIALS

- 2 DPNs or a pair of circular needles

### NEW ABBREVIATIONS

**brp:** brioche purl, i.e. purl a stitch together with its yarn over
**LC:** light colour
**DC:** dark colour

## Instructions

2-colour brioche is a 4-row pattern and is worked as follows:

**Row 1:** Worked on the RS with LC.
**Row 2:** Also worked on the RS, but using DC. This means that after having completed the first row, you need to slide the sts back to the other end of the needle (hence the need for circular needles or DPNs) and knit again with the other yarn, turn.
**Row 3:** Worked on the WS using the LC. Do not turn at the end of this row. Slide the sts to the other end of the knitting needle.
**Row 4:** Worked on the WS using the DC.
These 4 rows are repeated throughout. Brioche sts are knitted on Rows 1 and 4, but purled on Rows 2 and 3.

It sounds complicated, but once you get the hang of it it makes perfect sense!

Using MC, cast on 25 sts.

**Row 1 (WS):** P1, [sl1yo, k1] to last 2 sts, sl1yo, k1, turn.
**Row 2 (RS):** With LC, sl1p, [brk, sl1yo] to last 2 sts, brk, bring LC to front, sl1p, do not turn. Slide sts to other end of needle.
**Row 3 (RS):** With DC, k1, [sl1yo, brp] to last 2 sts, sl1yo, k1, turn.
**Row 4 (WS):** With LC, sl1p, [brp, sl1yo] to last 2 sts, brp, bring LC to front, sl1p, do not turn. Slide sts.
**Row 5 (WS):** With DC, k1, [sl1yo, brk] to last 2 sts, sl1yo, k1.
**Rows 6–57:** Repeat Rows 2–5 another 13 times. Take care not to wrap the LC yarn around the selvedge!

Break LC yarn. Cast off with DC very loosely and weave in ends.

As with **48.** The Squishy One, this square should be joined sideways to the rest of the squares.

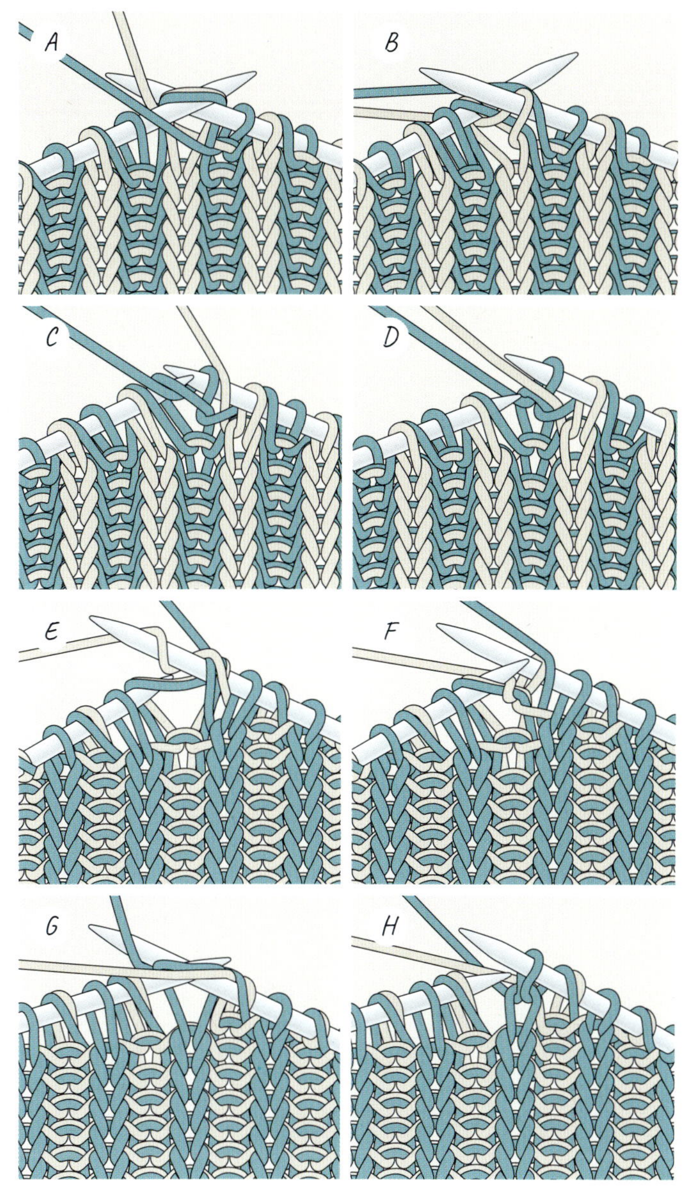


## Single pass brioche

Two-colour brioche can be worked with both colours simultaneously, working two rows in a single pass. This means you don't need to slide the stitches back every other row.

The front and back side rows are worked differently but are confusingly similar. It helps me to think that if I am working a double stitch, I should also end up with a double stitch, while single stitches remain single after they have been knitted.

As with double knitting, I always place the knit-stitch colour to the right. This means I switch the position of the yarns when I turn the work.

**To work a single pass right side row:** purl the selvedge stitch with the DC. Next, place the two yarns on your left index finger with the knit-stitch colour (the LC) on the right and under the DC. Hold DC down in front of LH needle and brk with the LC **(A)**. Come out under the DC to make a yarn over **(B)**. Purl the next stitch with the DC **(C)**. When completing this stitch, bring the needle up behind the LC **(D)**. When you come to the last stitch, bring LC to front. Knit last stitch with the DC. Turn to work a wrong-side row.

**To work a single pass wrong-side row:** purl the selvedge stitch with the DC. Place the yarns with the DC on the right. Purl double stitch with LC **(E)**, coming up between the two yarns, thus making a yarn over **(F)**. Hold LC in front of the LH needle tip **(G)** and knit it together with the next stitch using the DC **(H)**. When you get to the last stitch, bring LC to front. Knit last stitch with the DC. Turn.

### GEEKY NOTES 

Believe me, brioche looks so much more impressive if the knit stitches on the right side are in the lighter colour. That is why many brioche patterns use the terms "light colour" and "dark colour" instead of "main" and "contrast" colour.

**NOW YOU KNOW HOW TO**

knit two-colour brioche

See clips 50.1, 50.2

# 50. The Sophisticated One

## *How to make brioche decreases*

Really impressive patterns can be made using brioche increases and decreases. However, to keep an uninterrupted sequence of brioche knit and purl stitches, you need to add or decrease two stitches at a time, making these increases slightly more complicated than regular ones.

### YOU ALREADY KNOW HOW TO

- cast on, knit, and cast/bind off (**00**. The Basic One)
- slip the first stitch purlwise (**01**. The Slippy One)
- purl (**03**. The Purly One)
- follow a knitting pattern containing abbreviations (**04**. The Seedy One)
- decrease by knitting two stitches together (**06**. The Mitred One)
- make a yarn over (**07**. The Holey One)
- make a left-leaning decrease (**08**. The Left One)
- make a double decrease with the middle stitch at the bottom (**13**. The Loopy One)
- work "make one" increases (**14**. The Neat One)
- make increases and decreases on purl rows (**15**. The Complicated One)
- knit in the round (**16**. The Circular One)
- knit brioche (**48**. The Squishy One)
- knit two-colour brioche (**49**. The Accented One )

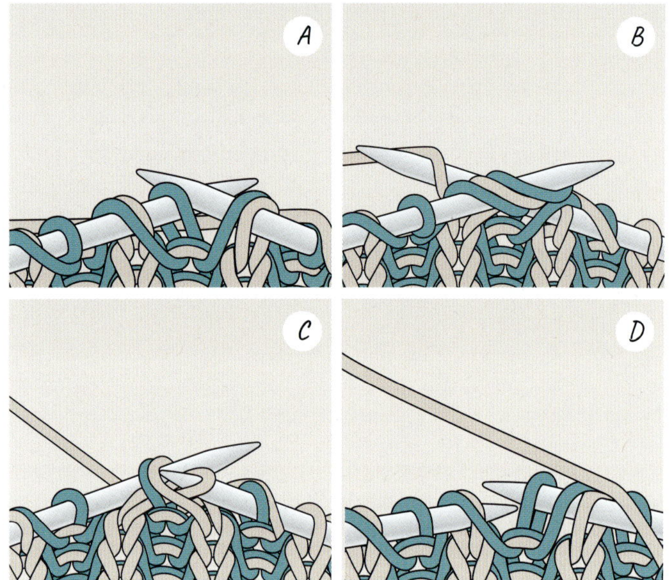


### EXTRA MATERIALS

- yarn in 2 different colours
- circular needles, 4mm (US size 6 or UK size 8), 40cm/16in long
- 5 DPNs, 4mm (US size 6 or UK size 8)
- 4 stitch markers, one of which should be different to the rest to mark the beginning of the round

### NEW ABBREVIATIONS

**brLsl dec:** brioche left-slanting decrease
**brRsl dec:** brioche right-slanting decrease

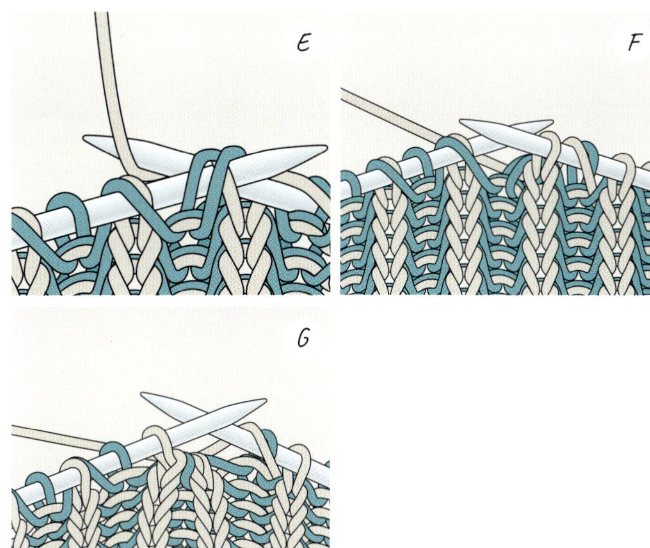


## Anna's tips...

- I like to use single-pass brioche whenever I have a pair of rows without increases or decreases. For rows/rounds with decreases, I revert to normal brioche, working one colour at a time.
- If you use single-pass brioche in this square, remember that you are always on the right side when knitting in the round, so all rounds will be the same.

## Instructions

Using circular needles and DC, cast on 108 sts. Join in the round and PM to mark the beginning of the round. Take care not to twist your stitches.

**Rnd 1:** Purl, PM after every 27th st.
**Rnd 2:** [SSK, k to 2 sts before marker, k2tog, SM] 4 times. (8 sts decreased)
**Rnd 3:** Purl.
**Rnd 4:** As Rnd 2. (92 sts)
**Rnd 5:** [Purl to marker, M1L, SM] 4 times. (96 sts)
**Rnd 6:** With LC, [k1, sl1yo] to end of round.
**Rnd 7:** With DC, [sl1yo, brp] to end of round.
**Rnd 8:** With LC, [brk, sl1yo] to end of round.
**Rnd 9:** As Rnd 7.
**Rnd 10:** With LC, *brLsl dec, sl1yo, [brk, sl1yo] to 4 sts before marker, brRsl dec, sl1yo, SM**. Repeat from * to ** another 3 times. (16 sts decreased)

**To work a brLsl dec:** sl a brk st **(A)**, k the next brk st together with the p st **(B)**, pass sl st over **(C)**.

**To work a brRsl dec:** make a SSK, i.e., sl a brk st knitwise, sl the purl st knitwise **(D)** and k them together through the back loops **(E, F)**. Sl this st back to the LH needle and pass the following brk st over it **(G)**. Sl the st back to the RH needle.

**Rnds 11–30:** Repeat Rnds 7–10 another 5 times. (16 sts)

Transfer the sts to DPNs as you decrease.

**Rnds 31–34:** Repeat Rnds 7–9 once more.
**Rnd 35:** With LC, [BrLsl dec, sl1yo] 4 times. (8 sts)
**Rnd 36:** With DC, [sl1yo, brp] 4 times.

Break both yarns and pass the DC through the remaining sts. Pull the yarn to close the hole tightly and weave in the ends.

## GEEKY NOTES

### Why all this fuss for a brioche decrease?

Because you need to bind off two stitches at the same time, making sure that the middle stitch lies at the bottom of the decrease, underneath the two knit stitches.

### How are brioche increases worked?

For a single brioche increase, you need to make two new stitches: a brioche knit stitch and its neighbouring brioche purl stitch, so the kyok double increase is used. For multiple increases, you work kyokyok, kyokyokyok etc., always making sure to produce an odd number of stitches. Because these increases are worked in a brioche stitch they are called brkyobrk, brkyobrkyobrk, etc., respectively.

# MAKE THE BLANKET

# PLACEMENT

In the chart you can see how I have placed the squares, but you can change the placement if you want, as long as you follow certain guidelines.

All squares have more or less the same width, but they differ in height. The squares can be divided into five groups:

Group A – the shorter squares: 1, 2, 4, 13, 24, 39, 42.

Group B – the taller squares: 3, 5, 7, 8, 9, 10, 11, 12, 14, 15, 20, 21, 25, 26, 27, 30, 32, 33, 34, 35, 36, 40, 41, 45, 46, 48, 49.

Group C – the square ones, i.e., the ones knitted in the round and **37.** The Logged One: 16, 17, 18, 19, 28, 29, 31, 37, 38, 43, 44, 50.

Group D contains only one square: **06.** The Mitred One, which I like to place in the corners of my blanket.

Squares within each group are more or less interchangeable.

Squares 22, 23 and 47 can be combined with squares of any group.

The grids on this page show how I have placed the squares in the two blankets: the full size throw **(A)** and the baby blanket **(B)**.

A

| | | | | | | |
|---|---|---|---|---|---|---|
| 6 | 4 | 1 | 42 | 1 | 13 | 6 |
| 34 | 26 | 35 | 32 | 15 | 20 | 9 |
| 40 | 7 | 47 | 49 | 22 | 30 | 21 |
| 35 | 22 | 28 | 48 | 50 | 23 | 7 |
| 8 | 16 | 44 | 29 | 43 | 17 | 15 |
| 27 | 38 | 18 | 37 | 19 | 31 | 36 |
| 3 | 23 | 12 | 3 | 11 | 47 | 10 |
| 5 | 14 | 41 | 33 | 25 | 45 | 46 |
| 6 | 2 | 1 | 24 | 1 | 39 | 6 |

B

| | | | | |
|---|---|---|---|---|
| 6 | 2 | 42 | 39 | 6 |
| 14 | 11 | 23 | 12 | 5 |
| 9 | 19 | 37 | 18 | 10 |
| 21 | 3 | 22 | 15 | 20 |
| 8 | 16 | 31 | 17 | 7 |
| 6 | 13 | 4 | 1 | 6 |

To get a smooth outer edge, I place Group A squares along the top and the bottom, Group B squares with a garter-stitch border along the sides, and a mitred one in each of the four corners. I try not to mix squares of different groups in the same row and I do not place Group A squares next to Group B squares.

Squares like **26.** The Magic One, **33.** The Ropey One, **48.** The Squishy One, and **49.** The Accented One are not suitable for the outside border.

Take particular care where you place squares **24.** The Mosaic One and **42.** The Short One. These are short and not very stretchy heightwise, so they may distort your blanket. I place them in the middle of the row or symmetrically to each other, and definitely not in a row with taller squares.

One small thing I do is to turn the squares of the top row upside down. That way, I have cast-on edges both at the top and the bottom of my blanket.

My blanket is more or less monochrome, but if your squares are in many different colours, you may also want to take colour placement into account.

# JOINING THE SQUARES

The finishing stage in a project often affects the overall look and requires particular attention. Even advanced knitters often have to redo the finishing seams multiple times before they get them right. So, be patient with yourself and don't give up...

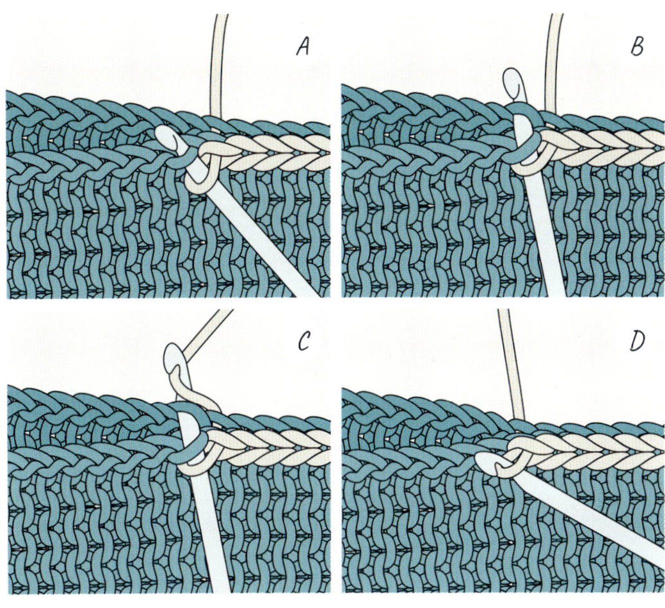


There are many different ways to join knitted squares. You can sew, crochet or even knit them together. My preferred method is to crochet them together with slipstitches. It is stretchier than sewing and easier than knitting them together – and it's much easier to undo, if needed.

Most of the squares have 27 stitches across and 24 slipped stitches on each side (1 slipped stitch for every 2 rows). You will notice that there is a chain across the top of each square and down the sides, and half a chain across the bottom (the cast-on edge).

You would think that if you have two sides with the same number of stitches, you can simply knit them together one to one. Unfortunately, that is not always the case. You'll be joining the right side of one square to the left side of the other, or the cast-on edge to the cast-off edge, so the selvedge stitches will be shifted by one row or half a stitch. I usually do the first three or four stitches and then check on the right side to see if they align before I continue.

I use a larger crochet hook than recommended for my yarn and crochet rather loosely to get the right tension. I've used a 5mm (US size 6 or UK size H-8) hook for these squares.

Place the squares right sides together and crochet through the two outer loops of the two chains **(A, B, C, D)**. On the cast-on edge, you only have one loop (= half a chain), so that is the one you will use.

If you are joining squares with a different number of stitches on the edge you will need to skip some stitches on the square that has the most stitches, and you need to distribute these skips evenly, i.e., if you have 27 stitches on one square and 24 on the other, you should skip three stitches on the "larger" side as follows: join the first six stitches one to one, skip one stitch on the square with 27 stitches, join next six stitches one to one, skip one stitch, join next six stitches, skip one, join the remaining six stitches.

When joining the squares, I first do the vertical lines and then the horizontal ones in one continuous line per row or column.

A skein of 50g (100m/109yds) was more than enough to assemble the baby blanket consisting of 30 squares (5 x 6). For the big blanket consisting of 63 squares (7 x 9) I used approximately 60g of DK yarn (120m/130yds).

# WASHING AND BLOCKING

After completing a project, I always wash it for two reasons:

- most yarns are chemically treated. You should wash these, together with any dust or dirt accumulated during knitting, out of your project;
- washing knitted fabrics can even out irregularities. Some yarns even "bloom" when washed, i.e., they grow (slightly) in volume, making your fabric squishier and more even.

Wash using a wool detergent. Rinse well, changing the water a couple of times. Press excess water out of the project. Roll it in dry towels once or twice to get even more water out of it. Dry flat on a horizontal surface. This blanket is too large for most towels, so I use a couple of sheets instead.

Knitted fabrics are very forgiving, especially if made with yarn using stretchy materials like wool or acrylic. They can – to a certain extent – be stretched to the desired dimensions using pins or blocking combs while drying. This is called "blocking".

Stocking-stitch sections can be lightly steamed with an iron. Do not press hard – let the steam do the work. Do not press the more textured patterns like garter stitch, ribbing or moss stitch.

# WHAT NEXT?

My aim with this book is to take you through the techniques you are likely to encounter in a knitting pattern, and to give you my small tips and tricks, which knitting patterns do not usually include.

I believe that upon completion of this blanket, you can consider yourself a pretty advanced knitter.

Obviously, there are infinite interesting techniques and patterns out there, and they cannot all be covered in any single book. There are a few that I didn't manage to squeeze into a blanket square, but which I suggest you explore on your own. These are:

- More brioche. In this book, I've only covered the basic brioche stitch and the simple decreases, but there are such amazing patterns in brioche that I would highly recommend further exploring this amazing stitch.
- The Italian cast off. This is a very neat and stretchy sewn cast off, closely related to the grafting stitch, which you encountered in **41.** The Minimalist One. It obviously takes more time to do than a regular cast off, but is well worth the trouble for certain projects.
- Judy's Magic Cast-On is often used when knitting toe-up socks, and results in a completely seamless toe – the equivalent to the grafting stitch on top-down socks.
- The Icelandic cast off, which is less tight than the regular cast off, and therefore particularly well suited to garter stitch.
- Steeking. With this technique, you knit a sweater in the round and then cut it up to make a cardigan. That you would take a pair of scissors and cut up several weeks' or months' worth of knitting is a terrifying thought, but if you are doing stranded colourwork it's soooo nice not to have to purl. There are several different steeking techniques. Some people crochet the edges to prevent them unravelling. I prefer making a couple of seams on each side of the steek with the sewing machine before cutting. You may want to try steeking a sample or a small item, e.g., a mug cosy or a doll's sweater, before taking the big step.
- Correcting mistakes. These squares are rather small, so, in most cases, it will probably be easier to frog the square than to spend time trying to remedy the situation. However, if you are making a larger project, you will probably not want to undo many hours' worth of work for a single mistake. As you gain experience, you'll get used to "reading" the stitches and the construction of the fabric, which will make correcting mistakes easier.

😉 *And my last golden pieces of advice*

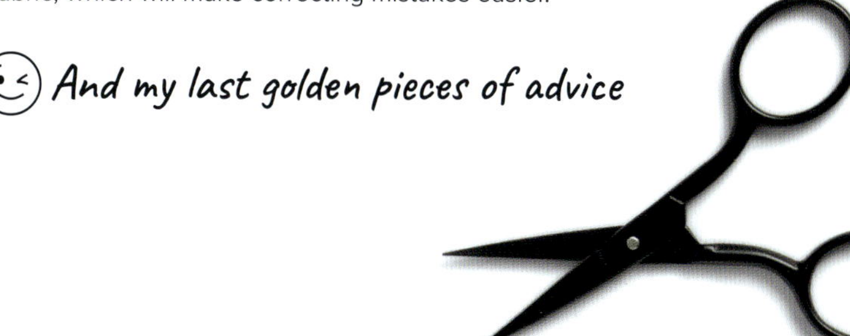

*For you:*

*Read instructions carefully through before starting any project.*

*Be consistent. Even a mistake becomes a "feature", if you're consistent. If you are inconsistent, even "correct" techniques will look wrong.*

*Enjoy every single stitch, even the ones you have to undo. Remember that mistakes and corrections are an essential part of the creative process* ✨

# ABOUT THE AUTHOR

Anna Pantelous has been knitting since early childhood. She describes herself as a 'Euromix' – she is half Greek and half Danish, and now lives in Belgium, where she knits and plays the trumpet in her free time. She discovered that social media is the perfect medium for spreading the joy of knitting, and for teaching visual learners how to knit.

**Follow Annaplexis on social media:**

You are very welcome to share your work on social media and to tag me **@annaplexis.knits** on Facebook, Instagram and Threads, **@annaplexis** on TikTok, Mastodon, tumblr and YouTube, **@annaplexis.bsky.social** on Bluesky. I'd love to see your work!

Photographer: Stavros Kanakaris

*A book like this one is not a solo project, even though there's only one name on the cover. I've had the privilege of working with an amazing professional team.*

*Thank you, Sarah, for encouraging me and trusting me to write this book. Thank you, Victoria and Rachael, for keeping everything on track. It's been a real joy working with you.*

*Thank you, Kang, for your amazing work and your patience. Thank you, Anna and Jess, for making it all look so good. And finally, thank you to everyone working behind the scenes, whom I didn't have the chance to meet.* ✨👏

# SUPPLIERS

## Yarn

Rico Design

www.rico-design.com

Rico Design GmbH & Co. KG
Industriestraße 19 – 23
33034 Brakel
Germany

## Equipment

The ring used in the colourwork videos is the Sterling Silver Drop Ring by Katerina Roukouna:

roukouna.com/products/drop-sterling-silver-ring

8, G. Zografou Str.
15 772 Zografos, Athens, Greece
Tel: +30 2107704022

# INDEX

A DAVID AND CHARLES BOOK
© David and Charles, Ltd 2025

David and Charles is an imprint of David and Charles, Ltd
Suite A, Tourism House, Pynes Hill, Exeter, EX2 5WS

Text and Designs © Anna Pantelous 2025
Layout and Photography © David and Charles, Ltd 2025

First published in the UK and USA in 2025

Anna Pantelous has asserted her right to be identified as author of this work in accordance with the Copyright, Designs and Patents Act, 1988.

All rights reserved. No part of this publication may be reproduced in any form or by any means, electronic or mechanical, by photocopying, recording or otherwise, without prior permission in writing from the publisher.

No part of this book may be used or reproduced in any manner for the purpose of training artificial intelligence technologies or systems without permission from David and Charles Ltd.

Readers are permitted to reproduce any of the designs in this book for their personal use and without the prior permission of the publisher. However, the designs in this book are copyright and must not be reproduced for resale.

The author and publisher have made every effort to ensure that all the instructions in the book are accurate and safe, and therefore cannot accept liability for any resulting injury, damage or loss to persons or property, however it may arise.

Names of manufacturers and product ranges are provided for the information of readers, with no intention to infringe copyright or trademarks.

A catalogue record for this book is available from the British Library.

ISBN-13: 9781446315125 paperback
ISBN-13: 9781446315149 EPUB

This book has been printed on paper from approved suppliers and made from pulp from sustainable sources.

Printed in China through Asia Pacific Offset for:
David and Charles, Ltd
Suite A, Tourism House, Pynes Hill, Exeter, EX2 5WS

10 9 8 7 6 5 4 3 2 1

Publishing Director: Ame Verso
Publishing Manager: Jeni Chown
Senior Commissioning Editor: Sarah Callard
Editor: Victoria Allen
Project Editor: Rachael Prest
Designer: Anna Wade
Pre-press Designer: Susan Reansbury
Illustrations: Kuo Kang Cheng
Art Direction: Jess Pearson
Photography: Jason Jenkins
Production Manager: Beverley Richardson

Video tutorials are available to watch free from www.bookmarkedhub.com. Search for this book by the title or ISBN: the files can be found under 'Book Extras'. Membership of the Bookmarked online community is free.

David and Charles publishes high-quality books on a wide range of subjects. For more information visit www.davidandcharles.com.

Share your makes with us on social media using #dandcbooks and follow us on Facebook and Instagram by searching for @dandcbooks.

Layout of the digital edition of this book may vary depending on reader hardware and display settings.